# Social Networking
# *for* ROOKIES

## Titles in the *for* ROOKIES series

*Dealing with Difficult People for Rookies* by Frances Kay
*Emotional Intelligence for Rookies* by Andrea Bacon & Ali Dawson
*Generation Y for Rookies* by Sally Bibb
*Job Hunting for Rookies* by Rob Yeung
*Low-Budget Marketing for Rookies* by Karen McCreadie
*Negotiation Skills for Rookies* by Patrick Forsyth
*NLP for Rookies* by Rebecca Mallery & Katherine Russell
*Social Networking for Rookies* by Tina Bettison
*Time & Stress Management for Rookies* by Frances Kay

## About the author

**Tina Bettison** is an observer of and a writer about people, their motivations, their behaviours and their connections. Her own network is diverse and eclectic and she just about always knows "someone who can...". She still considers herself to be a rookie in the world of networking and social media, but thinks she's getting the hang of it now. In addition to *Social Networking for Rookies*, Tina has written three books of horsey humour and likes to ponder and blog about what really drives consumer behaviour. She is also a radio and TV presenter, horsewoman and shoe guru.

# Social Networking
## *for* ROOKIES

Copyright © 2009 LID Editorial Empresarial and Marshall Cavendish Limited

First published in 2009 by

Marshall Cavendish Limited
Fifth Floor
32–38 Saffron Hill
London EC1N 8FH
United Kingdom
T: +44 (0)20 7421 8120
F: +44 (0)20 7421 8121
sales@marshallcavendish.co.uk
www.marshallcavendish.co.uk

A member of **BPR**

businesspublishersroundtable.com

Marshall Cavendish is a trademark of Times Publishing Limited

Other Marshall Cavendish offices: Marshall Cavendish International (Asia) Private
Limited, 1 New Industrial Road, Singapore 536196 • Marshall Cavendish Corporation.
99 White Plains Road, Tarrytown NY 10591–9001, USA • Marshall Cavendish International
(Thailand) Co Ltd. 253 Asoke, 12th Floor, Sukhumvit 21 Road, Klongtoey Nua, Wattana,
Bangkok 10110, Thailand • Marshall Cavendish (Malaysia) Sdn Bhd, Times Subang, Lot 46,
Subang Hi-Tech Industrial Park, Batu Tiga, 40000 Shah Alam, Selangor Darul Ehsan,
Malaysia

A CIP record for this book is available from the British Library

ISBN 978-0-462-09954-5

Illustrations by Nuria Aparicio and Joan Guardiet

Printed and bound in Great Britain by
TJ International Limited, Padstow, Cornwall

# Contents

# Introduction

It's a small world, and with the advent of online networks it's getting smaller. Now we can talk to just about anyone, anywhere, anytime. Who you know has always been as important as what you know, and social or business networks (that is, groups of people connecting together with a common interest) have existed since time began. Your connections are instrumental in everything from business deals or career progression to finding the best restaurant or beach to visit on holiday. The spread of the internet and the rise of offline and online networks for all manner of interests have spawned a whole new way of making connections. Social networking is changing the way we meet people, make friends and do business. If you aren't connecting or connected, you lose out to those who are.

Researchers at Microsoft recently revealed results of a study into the theory of six degrees of separation, which suggests that we are never more than six people away from the person we want or need to connect with. The research database of 30 billion messages covered all of the Microsoft Messenger instant-messaging network, or roughly half of the world's instant-messaging traffic, for June 2006. For the purposes of the study, two people were considered to be acquaintances if they had sent one another an instant message. Examining the

2

minimum chain lengths it would take to connect all the users in the database, the researchers found that the average length was 6.6 steps and that 78 per cent of the pairs could be connected in seven links or fewer.

This interconnectedness has particular relevance for social networking. While most of us think of social networking as teenagers playing around on Facebook, it is in fact *the* way forward in building your connections, both social and business. If you are only ever six people away from the one you want to meet, then tapping into and building good networks is the way to reach that person faster and more effectively. And of course you are the person whom someone else wants to meet, so your network is not just of value to you, it is of great value to others too. Technology now available through mobile and internet networks makes it supremely easy to reach those connections.

Social networks and social networking cover a wide spectrum and encompass many different ways of engaging with other people. As well as the typical and well-known "fun" networks, there are social/business networks, specific interest networks, online communities and clubs, forums, niche networks and blogs. These are the tools of engagement and connection in the networking world.

How you use them depends on your strategy (which we'll cover in Chapter 2) and some are more appropriate than others. For example, you might use a "fun" network for connecting with others who share similar leisure interests in music and movies or cult TV programmes. For business or career connections you need to join networks with a business or industry-specific focus. Social networking is used for a multitude of things: meeting new people, sharing information, asking for help and advice, market research, marketing, profile raising, publicity, promotion and increasingly in the political arena for getting closer to the voters.

In the USA, for example, Barack

Obama, in pursuing the 2008 Democratic presidential nomination, set up his own social network. Supporters could post their profile and blog on the site, and network with other like-minded people both online and at local events. Supporters could also create and join groups on the site and invite their friends to join. It was a great way to build campaign momentum and to engage people at the grassroots level. Politicians the world over are now using social networking and blogging as a way to reach their constituents, in order to appear more accessible and to raise their profile.

Social networking is also probably the most important tool for authors wanting to promote their books and gather a following of dedicated fans. Similarly bands and musicians have to have a profile and their music on the networks that their fans visit. Social networks are critical for new, and especially independent, bands, otherwise they have no following at all. Even large companies are now trying to develop social media strategies and have a brand presence on the networks they think their customers inhabit.

So social networking is definitely something you need to embrace, but leaping in without a plan is not recommended. It is important to know your purpose in networking and to choose the right sites for your purpose. We'll take you through the minefield of choosing the right sites in Chapters 3 to 5.

You need to be aware that there is etiquette to using online sites, just as there is in the "real" world. You wouldn't launch into a sales pitch without getting to know something about the other person if you were meeting them face to face for the first time, so it's not acceptable online either (though we do have a way of dealing with that in Chapter 4 should it happen to you).

Online networking is not a substitute for meeting face to face. We always feel more connected to someone if we have met them, and most business is done between people who know and trust each other. Social networking is about building

4 relationships and building trust. It is as much about what you can give as it is about what you can get. Offering your expertise to help your contacts, and giving it freely, really helps build your connection with them.

Asking for help is a good way to build your connections too. The experts you want to know are usually happy to share their knowledge and expertise, and often this is the kind of advice that money just cannot buy. In the process they frequently introduce you to other very useful people, who you wouldn't otherwise get to know.

What is important to you in developing your network? Do you want just to meet like-minded people, or do you want to build a significant profile via social networking? In the first chapter we will take an overview of the different types of sites and networking tools available and what you can do with them. In Chapter 2 we'll show you how to define your short, medium and long term networking goals and how to create your strategy and tactics for achieving them.

There are so many options, and it is easy to get overwhelmed and lose sight of what you really want to focus on. The aim of this book is to cut through that "overwhelm" and help you develop a clear purpose and strategy for your social networking success.

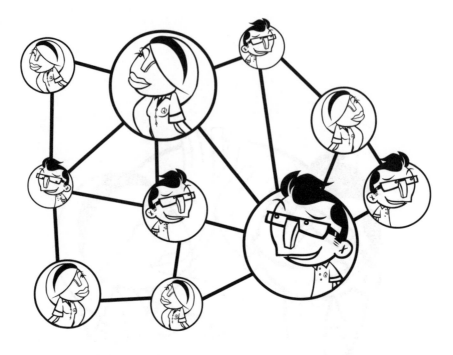

The purpose of this chapter is to give you an overview of social net-working, and to help you understand the different types of networks available and the different ways you can use them. There are literally hundreds of groups and networks you can join for a variety of reasons: social connections with friends and family, meeting new people, build-ing business contacts, sharing information, shared interests, market research, marketing your business and so on.

# CHAPTER 1

# Getting to know your networks

## *Types of networks*

You are probably familiar with, or at least have heard of, Facebook and MySpace, and you might think these are what social networking is all about. They are probably the best known, but they certainly aren't the only networks around. Wikipedia has a list of the most popular and well known general social networking sites, at http://en.wikipedia.org/wiki/List_of_social_networking_websites.

Each site listed also has its own page on Wikipedia, which gives details of the site and what it offers. This is a useful resource and well worth the visit. Another useful resource is http://findasocialnetwork.com/search.php. Here you can type in your interest and the site will give you all the networks, groups and communities in its database related to that subject.

# 8    Fun/friends

These networks are open to anyone, anywhere, and are for general interest. They include Facebook, MySpace, Bebo, Badoo, Bahu, Buzznet, Flixster and Flickr, and the list goes on. Some are more focused towards personal profiles and sending messages to your friends, others are for sharing photos, music, and journals. For example, Buzznet members participate in communities that are created around ideas, events and interests; most predominantly, music, celebrities and the media. Facebook members share their interests through their profile and write messages on friends' "walls". They can also challenge friends to quizzes and other games. In most of these networks you can join or form special interest groups.

In most cases there are different levels of privacy for your information, so that it is not open to public view and can only be accessed by friends and connections. These sites have been most popular with young people under 25, but that is shifting as more mature users join to keep in touch in friends and family.

Chapter 3 looks in depth at these fun networks for social connecting, including the do's and don'ts and what you need to be aware of when you use them for connecting with other business colleagues.

## Social/business and professional/business

Networks under this category by their very nature attract business and professional people rather than teenagers and college students. The most well known are LinkedIn, Xing and Ecademy, all of which have a multinational following and members from around 200 countries.

The social/business networks encourage connecting on a social basis from which you build business relationships. The professional/ business networks are aimed more towards making specific connections for referring business. Both are useful in building your business connections and your reputation in your field. Most of these networks include the opportunity to have an extensive profile, write your own blog on the site, and join groups of interest. Some enable more

privacy than others, but the point of these sites is to be seen and
found online.

Chapter 4 gives you more information about building business connections, the popular sites and how to get the best from them.

## Interest specific communities

These groups tend to operate through special interest membership sites, message boards and forums. Some have profiles, some don't. The purpose of these sites is to bring together people who share a particular interest, for example art or poetry, sport or gaming. They may also be set up to provide specific support groups for people sharing similar life issues such as bereavement or illnesses.

The value of communities in social networking is that you can easily make connections with people with whom you share a common interest. If you regularly post on the message boards or blogs of these communities, then you start to become known and it helps to build your reputation and the number of people who know of you. Transferring these connections to other networks becomes easier when you are known and trusted.

## Niche networks

It is becoming increasingly popular to start up your own niche network. These are usually membership by invitation only (you can apply to join and the administrator decides whether to accept your application) to ensure that the group is topical and relevant. Niche networks have a very specific focus, which enables members to synergize with and leverage the brain power of like-minded individuals in a way which is harder to do in general interest networks. For a start you don't have to search for or attract like minds; you are immediately among them.

10     A niche network will generally have a small number of members – hundreds rather than thousands – so are they limiting? Perhaps not, as Andy Lopata, director of the online network Word of Mouse, comments on his blog (www. /networkingandreferrals.blogspot.com): "With so many networks fighting for less and less of our free time, it is the networks that draw you back time and again that will keep our attention. The large social networks, which have the critical mass to be talked about and referred to, will continue to grow and help people grow their network base. However, networks where you find people of a like mind, discussing the issues that are relevant to you and connecting you with the people who make a difference in your business, or your life, will draw people in more regularly."

### Rookie Buster

With so many networks fighting for less and less of our free time, it is the networks that draw you back time and again that will keep our attention.

# The many uses of social networking

## Building your social connections

If you are new to online networking, joining a fun social site where you can link up with and keep in touch with friends can be a good introduction and a place to get used to the etiquette. Purely social sites are good places to explore your interests and find new friends who share those interests with you. If you follow particular bands or have a love of a particular music genre, for example, you can join the band's fan club on sites like MySpace or Bebo or find others who share your passion for that music.

While this helps you navigate the world of social networks, it also gives you an opportunity to meet others who share your interests and

build relationships with them. Most relationships of any kind usually    11
start with finding common ground. Social sites are populated with
common interest; that is how they survive and thrive.

Social sites are good for keeping in touch with family and friends,
particularly if you are far apart (whether at opposite ends of the country
or on opposite sides of the world) and don't get to see each other often.
In one post (as opposed to several letters or emails) you can keep in
touch with what they are doing and keep them in touch with you. It is
a good way of reconnecting with old friends too, who you may have
lost touch with as they or you moved on in location or life.

An added benefit is that you can also connect with their friends,
because you have something in common with them, and that also
grows your network. In terms of the six degrees of separation referred
to in the introduction, it is most likely to be the friends of friends of
your friends who lead you to that one person you want to meet.

We don't tend to discuss business with friends and family, and quite
often they have little idea what we do on a daily basis. Posting blogs
and videos on to your "fun" network account can therefore be a useful
and unobtrusive way of letting people know what is happening in your
business life.

### Rookie Buster

It is most likely to be the friends of friends of your
friends who lead you to that one person you want to meet.

Equally your "fun" network can be a useful way of letting your business and networking contacts know what you are like as an individual.
After all, people buy people, and if you can break down the barriers
imposed by business suits, you may fast-track some relationships.
Clearly you have to be careful that whatever you reveal does not compromise you or them. A general rule of thumb is that anything you are

12    not happy for your boss, business partner or mother to know about, does not find its way on to your profile!

## Building your business connections

There are a number of benefits to joining a business-focused network, whether you are in a large corporation or a one-man-band microbusiness.

Business networks are ideal for targeting the people you want to meet and asking your connections to introduce or refer you. The opportunities to meet face to face with more than a handful of decision-makers in your target industries are often limited to an annual conference and one or two professional association functions. Online, you can be highly focused in your networking strategy, which you can't do as effectively in person. Online business networks give you the opportunity to search for and locate people in a particular industry, role, and/or company, and find out what synergies you share before making contact.

**Rookie Buster**

Business networks are ideal for targeting the people you want to meet and asking your connections to introduce or refer you.

In person there is a limit to how many people you can meaningfully connect with in a given amount of time. Online business communities and blogs enable you to have public conversations, reaching many people with just one contact. This activity will raise your visibility and personal and company profile, helping you to identify potential partners, advocates and customers. Your entire network then becomes an extension of your business development team.

This is effectively low cost marketing and publicity for you. Some sites are free to join; others have nominal fees or a sliding scale of fees with increasing access to networking tools. You cannot actively participate in many sites, but you can passively have your profile listed on many so you can be found, and if these all have inbound links to your website, that helps your search engine rankings.

Special interest groups are part of the business networking scene. Creating a group around a topic related to your business is a great way to build credibility as a leading thinker in your field. On Ecademy (now ten years old) there are 4,540 clubs, ranging from the Brand Network (a forum designed for like-minded marketers to share ideas, experiences and beliefs in order to help them better shape and build the brands they work with) to the Malt Whisky Club (for those with a passion or curiosity for malt whisky, clearly). On Perfect Networker, a relatively new entrant launched in 2008, there are just over 100 groups.

When anyone joins a network, they put up their profile, look to see who else they know and then look for the groups they are interested in. If you form a group within a network, you are pretty much guaranteed a receptive audience and some immediate connections.

## Rookie Buster

If you form a group within a network, you are pretty much guaranteed a receptive audience and some immediate connections.

## 14 Using online networks for marketing and market research

Participating in groups and communities is a good way to learn about consumer interests. Posting carefully worded questions on discussion boards and blogs can elicit information and feedback that would be much harder and more costly to find out through focus groups or offline surveys. Just keeping your eyes and ears open and reading the blogs of others can give you a good steer as to the feedback on certain topics.

If you want a quantitative reaction to a question (meaning, how many people agree or disagree), then a poll is a good tool to use, and many networks have polls or surveys as standard on their sites.

Online networkers are usually pretty generous. If you want specific feedback on your products or services, your network will usually give you their honest opinion if you ask for it. Word your questions carefully to elicit the response you want. Getting feedback that your product sounds great is one thing. Would they pay what you want to charge for it and put their money where their mouth is, is another question entirely, but one you want an answer to before you invest heavily in a new product.

### Personal branding and publicity

Social networking can work well as part of your publicity strategy as an expert in your field. Your profile, blog and participation in discussions or forums gives you a much more accessible outlet than the media (who rarely read press releases, mostly because they get so many). It is also much more targeted publicity. Yes, it's great to have an article in the local newspaper, but is your target audience reading it? It's much easier to go direct to where your audience is and speak to them there. And if you make a point of giving generously with your expertise and saying something insightful, profound or controversial, you will get quoted and linked to.

Every network you join, every profile you have online, right down to the signature you add on your email, is an opportunity to reinforce your brand or your profile. Every time someone refers a colleague to your profile or forwards your email with your signature, it reinforces your brand and raises awareness of who you are and what you stand for. Your networking activity is the human voice behind your brand or your company. It is how you build trust and your reputation. It is your most powerful marketing tactic; people buy from people they like and trust.

### Rookie Buster

Every network you join, every profile you have online, right down to the signature you add on your email, is an opportunity to reinforce your brand or your profile.

If you have identified a narrowly defined target audience, the odds are good that you can identify a virtual community where it is already gathered, or, if it doesn't already exist, you can just create one, seed it with your closest relationships, and watch it grow. Word of mouth and advocacy are the best forms of marketing. We all know that a recommendation counts for a lot when trying out a new product, service, person or place. Social networks are beautiful breeding grounds for word-of-mouth marketing, as recommendations spread like wild fire. Cultivate your networks and your communities so they recommend you to theirs; and be sure to reciprocate with recommendations too. Social networks are two-way streets. You get back what you give out.

### Rookie Buster

Social networks are two-way streets. You get back what you give out.

16    Chapters 7 and 8 are dedicated to using social networks for personal branding, marketing and research, giving you an overview on how to use social networking appropriately and elegantly for this purpose.

## Information sharing

There is a number of ways in which social networking can be used to share information with others. A private blog, group or network is a good way of sharing confidential information, where the access is limited to the authors or members of the group and there is no visibility to the wider public. This is particularly useful for project teams working together but far apart geographically. Large companies may have their own intranets, but small companies or individuals working together collaboratively may not.

If you have information you just want to share with the world, without necessarily using it for publicity or personal promotion, then blogs and social networks are great ways of doing it. Sometimes we just have an urge to share that great restaurant we went to, the film that really touched us, a book that inspired us or websites we found useful. Social networking is as much about sharing snippets as it is about getting known and noticed.

**Rookie Buster**

Social networking is as much about sharing snippets as it is about getting known and noticed.

# *Beware the dark side*

There is a downside to social networking, which you need to think about as you embark on this new social journey. Everything that you put out online is visible to the whole world unless you specifically make it invisible. It's also there for ever, as old web pages never die; they just go into an archive. Even if you delete something or amend it, the original will still be there lurking somewhere in the deep recesses of the internet archive.

There are plenty of stories now about teenagers who were rejected from job or university applications because of their profiles on Facebook or MySpace, and business deals lost for the same reason. People have been fired from jobs because of jottings on their blog which their employers took exception to. In the following chapters there are some good guidelines for networking etiquette. The best test of all is "Would my employer/business partner/mother be happy to read this?" If not, don't do it. Better to be safe than sacked.

# Coach's notes

## Finding your flame

The real value in social networking is in creating attraction to yourself and your business and in making connections from that attraction. By "attraction" in this context, we're talking about people wanting to connect with you and you with them because you add value to each other in some way. Roger Hamilton, creator of Wealth Dynamics (www.wealthdynamics.org) talks about this attractive state as being in your "flame". It is a great metaphor to start your journey into social networking.

Imagine you are a candle – part of you is the flame, and part of you is the wax. When you are in your flame, leveraging on your talents and your expertise, shining brightly in your sphere of influence, you light up the world around you, and people are attracted to that light. When you are in your wax, doing the stuff that needs doing but which doesn't light your fire, you don't feel so great, life feels heavy and your light dims.

What social networking provides are places for you to display your flame, to show the world your talent and your expertise, to attract people to you because they either share your flame (in other words, your experiences and interests) and want to build a bigger, brighter fire with you, or because your flame is their wax and they need you.

So in preparation for the rest of this book, and particularly for the exercises in Chapter 2, you might want to think about what your flame consists of (the talents, expertise and interests you have that other people will be attracted to and want to connect with) and what things are in your wax that you might find help or support with in the connections you make. There is a crib sheet in the appendix at the back of the book for you to use if you wish.

**Go for it!** The English poet John Donne (1572–1631) wrote of human interconnection in his words "No man in an island, entire of itself; every man is a piece of the continent, a part of the main."

Donne knew that people are not isolated from each other, and that through their connections they contribute to the whole continent of life and affect each other's lives every day. Your social networking activity is just one thread in the overall web, but a vital thread nonetheless.

You might be wondering how you are going to affect other's lives beyond the obvious referrals through your network. You might offer support or advice, you might give testimonials and you might make someone think. Social networking is much more than gathering "friends" to "poke".

20

Notes

# Notes

Developing networks and connections both online and offline can be a time-consuming business. It's all too easy to sign up to particular networks because friends invited you, then simply grab any connection you can make and be swamped by yet more invitations, without any real focus and purpose. And it is easy to get swept up by the hype over certain social networking sites that may actually turn out to be detrimental to the reputation you want to build if you aren't focused in how you are using them. So this chapter focuses on focus – what you need to consider in developing your strategy for your social networking activity.

# CHAPTER 2

# Developing your social networking strategy

Without a purpose and a plan, you are going to get bogged down in the world of social networking. There are so many different networks with so many different angles that you need to give serious thought to what you want to get out of networking and what you want to give to it.

## Defining your purpose

You need to know what you're using a social networking site for. While it's OK to have a profile somewhere that's just for "hanging out", you need to know that hanging out is its purpose. If you are using a social networking site to try to build an audience, connect with other professionals, or meet a partner, it should be focused on achieving that end.

So what are you networking for? It's worth taking a moment and scribbling down some thoughts. Here are some ideas to get your thoughts flowing. Do you want to:

- Make new friends?
- Connect with current family and friends who you see only rarely?
- Meet people with shared personal interests?

24

- Meet people with shared business interests?
- Make connections with possible clients or business partners?
- Make connections with like-minded people in the same industry with whom you can discuss industry specific issues?
- Build your profile and reputation as the expert in your field?
- Promote your business, your brand, your book, your band?
- Put yourself "out there" as a potential job candidate?
- Research your market and find out what the world is saying about products and services in your industry?
- Join a like-minded community or build one?
- Inspire others?
- Share knowledge?

Once you have got some ideas as to your purpose, rank them in order of importance. What are your top three and which is the most important of those? That is the one to put the most focus on in building your strategy and in your networking activity.

# Setting your goals

Now you know why you are embarking on the social networking journey, it's time to set some goals for milestones along the way. Social networking activity takes time – not just the time you put into it, but the time it takes to build your network and start benefiting from it. Thomas Power, co-founder of Ecademy (www.ecademy.com), suggests that it takes one year to get known, another year to be liked and a third year to be trusted. So you should bear in mind that social networking is a long-term commitment, not a short-term quick fix.

**Rookie Buster**

Social networking is a long-term commitment, not a short-term quick fix.

Goals for year one might therefore include getting your profile
honed, joining one or two networks to test the waters, and starting a
blog. In year two you might look at expanding the networks you belong
to and exploring social bookmarking so that more people can find you
and your blog. In year three, now that you have built a more solid base
of contacts, you might think about creating your own niche network,
as some of your contacts will probably be keen to join you in a niche
of your own. You'll also want to break down your initial goals into
smaller goals that you are going to tackle each month, so that you don't
face being overwhelmed as soon as you start.

Here's an example to illustrate how you might set your own goals.
The **purpose**:

1.  Build a reputation for being the go-to professional in your field by
    giving good quality advice and help to others.
2.  Meet like-minded business professionals who can in turn...
3.  Introduce you to prospective clients.

Right now you have a website but no social networking presence.
So your **goals** are:

- Week 1: Find out which networks are used by your peers and
  other professionals with whom you want to connect.
- Week 2: Find out more about your existing customers, what they
  value in you and which networks they use.
- Week 3: Research other "names" in your industry and see what
  they are doing on the social networking scene.
- Week 4: Review other good blogs on your subject area.
- Week 5: Write a really good profile that showcases your talents
  and expertise in your field.
- Week 6 onwards: Join one network and aim to invite all your
  relevant personal contacts within one month of joining; aim to
  add one new contact each week whom you aren't already
  connected to. Aim to spend one hour every day on networking
  activity.
- Week 7 onwards: Start a blog so you can write about issues
  pertinent to your field of expertise – aim to post once a week to
  start with.

You may want to go into more detail on your own goals, but certainly write them down as *specifically* as you can; give yourself a way of *managing* your progress (in other words, knowing when you have achieved what you set out to do); make them *achievable* and *realistic* (social networking needs to fit in with your work/lifestyle); and put a *time frame* on them so you don't just drift along between sporadic bouts of activity.

The key to making social networking work for you is consistency and persistency, little and often. It has to fit with your way of working and your way of life, and it needs to be fun too – otherwise your best intentions will just fall by the wayside.

### Rookie Buster

The key to making social networking work for you is consistency and persistency, little and often.

# *Choosing your networks*

Having defined your purpose, choosing the appropriate networks and places to be seen is the next step. It can be tempting to sign up for dozens of social networking sites, especially when different friends and colleagues invite you to join the one they are using, but it's nearly impossible to make good use of a dozen different sites. Choose one or two sites and focus all your energies on creating useful, meaningful connections there.

## Building social connections

If your primary purpose is connecting with friends and family to share personal information and interests, then your networks should be chosen from the "social" sites. Having a primary business purpose doesn't stop you having a social site, but it does mean you don't want to focus too heavily on it and put too much time into it, so choose one that will make it easy for you to stick to your main purpose.

**Rookie Buster**

Having a primary business purpose doesn't stop you having a social site, but it does mean you don't want to focus too heavily on it and put too much time into it.

## Building business connections

If your primary purpose is a business-led one, then business networks are the place to focus. Having your profile on several is OK, but focus on one as your main place of connection and networking, at least to start with.

## Activity-specific communities and forums

These are often just message boards or forums without the full-on networking opportunities of social sites. However, they can be good places to build your profile or to join in a special interest group without spending too much time on adding friends and connecting. You connect simply by participating in the discussions. They are a good place to "sit in" on conversations for research.

## Niche networks

These are usually specific to an interest or topic, and are often by invitation only. They are good for meeting like-minded people and being part of a smaller and cohesive group. You may also decide to set up your own niche network, which is quite easy to do and a low-cost way of positioning yourself as a thought leader. It is certainly becoming a trend to set up a network around your niche.

## Blogs

A definite must if you are profile building, promoting, or seeking to gain attention for your thoughts and opinions. Chapter 6 is devoted to this subject. Deciding whether to blog, where to blog and how often to blog is a necessary part of your strategy. If your purpose is to raise your profile and share your expertise, you should certainly start a blog linked to your profile pages and encourage people to visit it and comment. It can be a big commitment, though, so be sure it is right for you before building it into your strategy.

**Rookie Buster**

Deciding whether to blog, where to blog and how often to blog is a necessary part of your strategy.

## Offline networking

Although most social networking takes place on the internet, you shouldn't forget that more business is still done following face-to-face meetings than purely online relationships. Meeting offline with people you meet online should be part of your strategy wherever possible.

# *Creating your profile*

Your profile is the most important part of your social networking and should be central to your strategy. It is the view that other people see of you – and their profile is what you see of them. Unless they know you well already it their first point of contact and the thing that lets them know you are someone they want to connect with. It is worth taking time to plan and carefully execute a great profile. You'd be surprised how many people never do this, though, and many don't put much thought into the About Me section. Putting effort into your profile will make you stand out from the crowd.

## Rookie Buster

Your profile is the most important part of your social networking and should be central to your strategy.

This is where the flame and wax exercise that you did at the end of Chapter 1 comes in useful. Your flame (your talents, expertise and interests) will form the main pillars of your profile.

When you visit someone's profile, what do you want to know about them? Are you more interested in their star sign or in their philosophy on life? What makes them interesting to you? What makes you want to connect with them? There are usually four things that attract you to making a connection with them:

- You get a sense of who they are.
- You understand what they do.
- You have something in common (interests, background, industry, philosophies, beliefs, values, etc.).
- You can see how you can add value to them and how they might add value to you and your network.

So when writing your profile think about who is going to read it

30 and what you want them to know about who you are, what you do, the expertise or knowledge you can contribute, your interests, background, philosophies, beliefs and values.

Write separate profiles for your business networks and your private ones. Keeping the two separate will make life easier, even if you have business connections that are also connected to you on a purely social fun site. Remember that your "friends" can usually see the profiles of your other friends/connections, and it might be on *their* profile not yours that the pictures of the two of you in an embarrassing situation appear. If your business colleagues were there too, then fine, but if that's not something you want to share with potential business partners, then best keep them apart. If necessary, create two profiles on the same site, one for your business persona, the other for your personal life; that way, instead of denying friend requests from friends and family, you can just refer them to the other profile.

Keep a copy of your profiles on your computer so you don't have to reinvent it every time you join a network. It's also a good idea to refresh your profile every few weeks, so there is always something interesting for your network to come back to. Life is dynamic, not static, so let your profile be dynamic too.

### Rookie Buster

Life is dynamic, not static, so let your profile be dynamic too.

Do be aware of the visibility of your profile. Don't put anything in there you would not want the world to know. Similarly, give careful consideration to photographs.

A picture is worth a thousand words, as the saying goes, and yet so few people put any effort into finding a good photo for their profile. A clear picture of yourself with a nice smile sends an instant message: it says "I am someone you can relate to."

Ideally it should be just a head shot, and particularly so on business networks. It is important that we can read each other's faces on a profile. Being able to look into someone's eyes, even in a photograph, establishes a sense of connection. Leave the pictures of a tiny you on a vast beach to your gallery or blog.

You only have a few seconds to be noticed, so make the most of those few seconds. A good picture will make you stand out from the crowd on the network. If necessary, get a professional to photograph you. You can use the image on all your profiles; it will be worth it.

Ken Rochon, founder of Perfect Networker (www. perfectnetworker.com), has this advice: "The surfer typically is looking for professionalism, attractiveness (as dictated by society for male and female potential contacts) and a sense of personality and friendliness. I've heard as much as 40 times more attention is spent on profiles with photos than without." He also suggests: "Do yourself another favour… keep your clothes on. People showing off their bodies in the social networking arena, intentionally or not, are difficult to take seriously with regard to business." It might seem obvious, but you would be surprised at the pictures some people post. If you want that kind of attention, best join a dating site.

There are more hot tips for creating the killer profile in Chapter 7 on Personal Branding.

## *Making connections*

You don't need to go wild and try to add everyone you know all at once. Give yourself a set amount of time each week for inviting friends and colleagues to join your network, for finding new people to connect with, for accepting invitations and giving them the courtesy of looking at their profile and sending them a message. Plan time for adding to your blog and participating in group discussions; allow twice as much time as you think it will take, but put a time limit on it, otherwise you can spend hours and hours on your networks.

32    Make your connections purposeful. Accept all invitations if you wish: you never know who might be able to connect you to that one person you want to meet. Random connections are often the ones that prove to be the most fruitful. In inviting connections to you, give some thought as to why you are extending the invitation and send a personal message with the invitation explaining why that connection is important to you. You'll generate a closer connection with that person if you do.

**Rookie Buster**

Accept all invitations if you wish: you never know who might be able to connect you to that one person you want to meet.

Most networks these days have a widget that will scan your address book and tell you if there's anyone you might already know on board. Some will recommend people you already know, places you've worked, or interests you've highlighted. If you come across someone you do actually know, no matter how distantly, add them. That is, after all, the point of social networking; to leverage the often-invisible connections that exist between us and other people. The worst that can happen is that they reject your invitation to connect, and that rarely happens.

## Give good value

As part of your strategy, think about what you will contribute, both in your invitations to connect and in your ongoing conversations. Say something useful, helpful or supportive. Share something of yourself, your thoughts, your opinions or your knowledge. If you aren't feeling inspired, then share a favourite quote, or a book you are reading, or a link to something you found interesting. The whole point of social networking is to connect *and* share.

Find a reason to connect with the people in your network; send them a message once in a while. The purpose of this is simply to keep a channel of communication open, so your message doesn't have to be profound. If you know when their birthday is, send them a brief "happy birthday" message. Even a clipping of news or a web-link you think will be of interest is fine. Make the message about *them*, not you.

Make it a part of your strategy to let people know why you're there, what your purpose is, and to reveal something of you. Give people a reason to pay attention to you. Most people in your network will stay in there indefinitely even if you don't do anything at all, but that is hardly the best use of a social network. Post something to your profile, front page, blog, wall, etc. every now and then, so that people learn something about you.

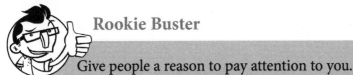

**Rookie Buster**

Give people a reason to pay attention to you.

## *Avoid clutter*

Many of the networks now have trillions of "apps" – applications for everything from sending cupcakes and throwing sheep to creating and adding business cards to your messages. It can be tempting to add lots of elements to your profile page, but if your page is so full of junk that nobody can see what is important about you, it defeats the purpose of it being a showcase for you. Limit yourself to only a couple of really useful extras, and keep your page clean and simple.

## Coach's notes

### Quick strategy checklist

1. Define your purpose – know what you want to get and to give.
2. Set your goals – short, medium and long term.
3. Find the right networks for you – where you can give and get what you want/need.
4. Create a great, attractive profile that shows you at your best.
5. Get connecting!

**Go for it!** Always remember that people are connecting to you as a person, not a job title. Penny Power, founder of Ecademy (www.ecademy.com), sums this up perfectly:

"Lets face it, what you *do* is not interesting. Sorry. Anyone can find a stranger in the telephone directory and buy from them. However *you* are interesting; you have all sorts of experiences, thoughts, vulnerabilities and ideas that make you fascinating. Your journey to this point in your life is interesting, and *why* you do what you do is interesting. All these factors lead to your expertise, to your passions, and that leads back to your business, and to you as a person who can be trusted and liked — and it leads to others caring about your success."

*Notes*

*Notes*

Networking is about building relationships, and generally we do business with people who we have already built a relationship with – even if that relationship has been built online. Many business relationships start out as social connections. Before the advent of the internet these social connections were created on the golf course and in clubs and communities, where you got to know each other because you shared an interest, and then business developed from it. Now we have the opportunity across the internet to network, share interests and build communities with people in countries and communities we may never visit in person.

# CHAPTER 3

# Building your social connections

## *Social connections aren't just social*

The "social" side of social networking is as important as making direct business contacts, precisely because it is through social connections that business connections are made and solidified. We tend to trust people more when we feel we know them, and getting to know them outside the business context helps build that trust. Consequently, when building social connections and using social sites to do so, it is important that you think about how your activity there will help build trust in who you are and what you do.

Consider your purpose and strategy for social networking from Chapter 2. How will building purely social connections help you achieve your aims? Here are some possibilities to consider:

### Revealing more of who you are

Building a profile on social sites enables you to show more of your social side, the interests you have outside work, the music you listen to,

40  the books you read, the charities you support, the sports you play or follow. These add to the roundedness of you as a personality; people can see you as a whole person, not just a one-dimensional business persona.

## Creating connection through shared interest

It is easier for people to make a first contact if they feel they have something in common with you. It is also easier for you to make contact with other people if you feel there is some synergy. Sharing an interest outside business gives you this common ground even if your business interests are different. If you have nothing in common, there is no glue to bind the relationship together, and the chances are that the contacts with no glue will just become names in your friends list rather than true relationship-building opportunities.

**Rookie Buster**

It is easier for people to make a first contact if they feel they have something in common with you.

## Creating connection for a common cause

Perhaps you support a specific charity or good cause. Connecting with other supporters can be a good way of doing more and finding out about other activities online or offline that you could be participating in. Supporting the same cause or charity can be very strong glue in developing trust in a relationship.

## Turning social connections into business contacts  41

Once you have made connections and started to build these relationships, you can start to use your network to further your business or career. Trying to sell directly to your contacts is not recommended if you want to keep their trust, but asking questions of them and sharing your needs is acceptable.

Use "Who do you know who ..." questions when you want to make a specific contact – for example, "Who do you know who has a contact in the HR department at company X?" or "Who do you know who might be interested in replacing their laptop?" Another example might be: "I want to move into a more senior position in my industry. Who do you know who might be looking for someone with my skill and expertise?"

### Rookie Buster

Use "Who do you know who ..." questions when you want to make a specific contact.

These are perfectly acceptable questions to ask of your social network, once you have got to know them and they you; and it's the most appropriate way of enabling them to be your business advocates as well as your friends.

## *Which sites are most appropriate for building social connections?*

If you put "lists of social networking sites" into Google or any other search engine, you'll find plenty of pages that give you lists of sites to browse. One good resource is findasocialnetwork.com/search.php: it allows you to search by subject and find just about every network you could possibly want to know about.

Whether you are into movies (www.flixster.com), sharing photos and videos (www.youtube.com, www.flickr.com, www.fotolog.com), meeting up again with old friends (www.friendsreunited.com), your pets (www.dogster.com, www.mycatspace.com, www.socialequine. com), your food (www.food.tv), social activism (www.care2.com), finding support as a young mother with children (www.cafemom. com) or joining a church (www.mychurch.com), there is a networking site out there for you!

Many of the general social networks started out as places for young people to meet and share photos, videos and their stories. Some of the general sites are still populated mostly by youngsters, so you need to be aware of the culture of the site you are joining. Will it fit with who you are and what you want to give and get from networking on that site? Some sites actually stipulate age restrictions and won't let you join if you are outside their age limits.

The best known general sites are Facebook, MySpace, Bebo and Badoo. Facebook and Badoo are for sharing information and lifestyle. MySpace and Bebo have staked their territory as more focused towards music, video and pop culture. In the search for a network to join, you really do have to research a few, get a feel for them and decide whether any of them is the right space for you.

## Deciding on the best ones for you

If you have done the exercises in Chapter 2 on defining your social networking strategy and goals, then you should have an idea of what you want to give, what you want to gain and how much time you have to put into it. It is important enough to say it again: social networking is time consuming, in both the time you spend actively participating and the time it takes for your network to get to know and trust you. Therefore join only those social networks that will support your strategy and that you have the time and willingness to participate in.

## Rookie Buster

Join only those social networks that will support your strategy and that you have the time and willingness to participate in.

It is worth making a note of your interests and deciding which of them you are most passionate about. For example, your list of interests might include reading, listening to music, wine tasting, going to the gym and photography; perhaps you also support cancer charities by doing an annual sponsored walk. Which of them would you really want to talk about with other people in your social networking activities?

If you are an avid reader and lover of books, you might want to join a network specifically for book lovers (such as www.shelfari.com or www.librarything.com). If music and bands are stronger interests, then networks related to that might be more appropriate (maybe www.myspace.com, www.lastfm.com or www.buzznet.com). If you are going to devote time to the network, it needs to be a network you *want* to devote time to.

## Rookie Buster

If you are going to devote time to the network, it needs to be a network you *want* to devote time to.

Each site has its own terms of use (usually found via a link at the bottom of the website) and most have community guidelines. I recommend that you read these on sites of interest before signing on. A general set of guidelines follows which will help you stay out of trouble in your chosen network.

# 44 *Guidelines for social networking etiquette*

Badoo (www.badoo.com) and CaféMom (www.cafemom.com) have the clearest sets of guidelines of all sites, and I've shamelessly stolen from them in putting together this list for you.

**Do follow the guidelines of each individual site; networks will delete your profile if you abuse their guidelines and rules. The guidelines here are a good rule of thumb, but not exhaustive. Most are common sense, but not always common practice.**

### 1. Respect other members
Social networks are diverse communities; respect for other people's beliefs and property must be made a top priority. You should behave in the same way on any site as you would in real life. Treat people as if you were talking to them face to face. You can be opinionated. You can be opposed to the ideas or opinions of others, and can say so. Discussion and debate are encouraged on most sites. However, if a healthy discussion breaks down into an exchange of attacks and insults or becomes too heated, leave it and report it to the site administrators so that they can take appropriate action.

### 2. Don't harass or personally attack others
When a discussion gets heated or involves a topic you feel passionate about, it's sometimes tempting to stop talking about the issues and instead talk about the people involved. Don't do it. If you must vent your feelings about another member, do it without identifying them, or, better still, do it on the privacy of a scrap of paper at home and then shred it. That way you get rid of your feelings without hurting those of others.

### 3. No bigotry, no stereotyping
Slurs, hate speech and attacks aimed at any race, colour, religion, national origin, disability or sexual orientation are not tolerated at all in networks and will be removed. Don't stereotype people; it isn't

acceptable. Report anyone who does to the site administrators. Networks need to be safe places for everyone involved.

### 4. No ganging up

You may not like everyone on your network, but don't harass someone or tell all your friends to go harass someone because you don't like something they said.

### 5. Expect to be challenged

If you're going to post something controversial, be prepared for others to disagree with you and your ideas. Expect your viewpoints and opinions to be vigorously questioned, challenged, and held up to scrutiny. If having your opinions challenged and being expected to defend your position will make you uncomfortable, don't post about that topic.

### 6. Keep it clean

Be respectful of others' sensibilities when posting in public areas any content that is adult in nature (either the topic or the manner in which you talk about it); better still, temper it so it is unlikely to cause offence.

### 7. Pictures: nothing borrowed, nothing blue

Do upload only your own photos and videos. Most sites take copyright very seriously. If you don't own the rights to a photo or video, don't post it. And don't post other people's photos as your own. Don't upload tasteless and pornographic photos, either; social networks are completely inappropriate places for such material. There is a fine line sometimes between a sexy photo and soft porn (for both sexes). If it might get you attention you don't want, don't upload it; and if that is the sort of attention you do want, then look for a more appropriate site.

## 8. Stay within the law

Don't do anything criminal, illegal or immoral, or encourage anyone else to do so. You will get reported. Any postings that network administrators reasonably believe or suspect are criminal or illegal in nature will be removed, and any conduct that they suspect is illegal or which poses a threat of illegal activity will be reported to the appropriate authorities. Networks do and will cooperate with authorities to prosecute anyone who breaks the law while using their site. Do not link to sites containing criminal or illegal activity either.

## 9. No spam

Don't spam and don't send "copy and paste" messages to other users. If you want to write someone a message, write a personal original message of your own.

## 10. Don't sell

Do not try to sell products, other sites, or yourself unless that has been explicitly allowed on the site; only post advertisements and promotions in designated areas or where allowed on a network. (But this may be quite different in a business network where promotion is actively encouraged. Make sure you know the rules on this for the site you are joining.)

Advertising could include, but is not limited to:

- Work at home businesses.
- Products that you are selling (personal or professional).
- Job opportunities.
- Charities and charitable causes.
- Promoting another website (personal, non-business websites are fine, anything else is not).
- Promoting your entry in a contest (e.g. "vote for my baby in the cutest baby contest on xyz.com").

Promotion is usually acceptable on your profile page, in areas designated as a "marketplace", in groups that allow advertising and promotion, and in messages to members who have explicitly asked for
information on a business.

### 11. Be careful with personal details

Don't share your personal information with someone unless you're
absolutely certain it is safe to do so, especially addresses and home
phone numbers. Online connections are not like face-to-face meetings, where you get a much stronger feel for whether you can trust that
person. Not everyone online is legitimate – though most are.

### 12. Imposters

If you suspect that someone on the site is an imposter or not legitimate, report the problem to the site administration team and let them
deal with it. Likewise do not pretend to be someone you are not.

### 13. Hold on to your wallet

Don't give money to people who ask for it online. While their stories
may move you, you have no way of knowing if they are legitimate.
Networks can't verify the identities of everyone on the site and you use
the site at your own risk.

### 14. Keep private stuff private

Don't share personal information about anyone else. Don't repost messages from private groups or messages in public places. If the information was posted in a private group, assume that the member wants it to
remain private.

## Coach's notes

### Six steps to getting connected

1. Take your list of interests and decide which ones you feel passionate enough about to want to share with others. Put your top two into findasocialnetwork.com/search.php and see which networks come up.

2. Research these networks. Read the terms of service and guidelines and study the About and Help sections. Do you have the right ethos for what you want? Will the people in this network be the right sort of people for you? The specialist social networks generally have more information about the types of people they want to attract to the network, which helps you decide if you are one of them.

3. Without joining up, if possible, browse some of the profiles and check out the groups and discussions. Many networks allow you access to a certain amount of information before you sign up. Make the most of this to check out it is the right place for you.

4. Having decided which is the network for you, join and put up your profile.

5. Start connecting by inviting friends you know well and who share your interest to join you there. It is always easier to start building your network with people you already know. You can begin to expand your contacts within the network by joining groups and participating in discussions. You'll soon find people asking to connect with you too.

6. Participate and make sure that you stay active in the communities you most value. Keep your profile updated. Comment on other people's work, link to other resources, participate in groups, and ask questions.

**Go for it!** As the poet W. B. Yeats said, "There are no strangers here, only friends you haven't yet met." Or to put it another way: "In a world of exaggerated differences, sharing a common interest counts for something. You could have the same problem, the same question, or the same hobby. If you knew these other people you could team up, collaborate, socialize, entertain or educate each other." (From Tony Effik's "Comments on the Social Graph" blog, socialgraph.blogspot.com.)

50

Notes

........................................................................................
........................................................................................
........................................................................................
........................................................................................
........................................................................................
........................................................................................
........................................................................................
........................................................................................
........................................................................................
........................................................................................
........................................................................................
........................................................................................
........................................................................................
........................................................................................
........................................................................................
........................................................................................
........................................................................................
........................................................................................
........................................................................................
........................................................................................
........................................................................................
........................................................................................
........................................................................................
........................................................................................
........................................................................................
........................................................................................
........................................................................................
........................................................................................
........................................................................................
........................................................................................
........................................................................................

*Notes*

Although some of the more generalist sites like Facebook are now adding business tools and applications, there is a strong selection of business-specific networking sites which are worth considering for your business networking needs. Unlike the mainly "social" sites, it is worth having a profile on several business sites even if you are only participating in one and are more passive on the others. When it comes to visibility for your business, more is more. This chapter is a guide to what you should look for in a business network and how to make the best use of it for you and your business.

# CHAPTER 4

# Building your business connections

## *Business networking opens up a dialogue*

Business networking sites are built by business people for business people, with the goal of establishing a community where business owners can connect with one another, get questions answered, ask for referrals, find employees (or employers) and foster new business relationships.

Even if you already have a website and a presence on the internet, it is a good idea to have a presence on the business networking sites too. You want as much exposure for your business as possible, and it is most likely that potential clients and employers are going to search your name or business on the internet. You want to make sure you are found, and with the profile that you want to display.

As we move into a new age of internet development, the aim is to be having a dialogue with your contacts and customers rather than the monologue of a static website. A website tends to be a passive business-development vehicle, letting you capture contacts that come to you (via your enquiries or "sign up" form), whereas business networking sites allow you to be proactive in reaching out to potential contacts and customers.

**Rookie Buster**

The aim is to be having a dialogue with your contacts and customers rather than the monologue of a static website.

Belonging to a network gives you the opportunity to build business relationships based on advocacy, referrals, collaboration, advice, inspiration, feedback and friendships. It lets you use your existing network to develop new partnerships. And it is a great way to glean advice on any subject relating to running a business.

# *Know what you want to give and to get*

Even more critical on a business network is your strategy for giving and receiving.

## Show your "flame"

A strong profile that showcases you and your business is a must to create the attraction you need to develop those contacts. Remember the flame/wax exercise from Chapter 1? This is where you really get a chance to show your flame – your talent, your expertise and what you have to offer and contribute.

# Ask for help

It is also your opportunity to ask for the help or advice you need (your wax), and the contacts you would like to meet. Drawing up a mind map of your business contacts can help you work out where the gaps are in your knowledge and the kinds of people it would be useful to be introduced to.

## Keep your profile current

It is most important that you regularly update your profile on these sites, as you will get a constant stream of new visitors, plus you want a reason for your network to revisit you. Adding snippets of information about projects you are working on or have completed (without breaking any confidentiality), or a tip of the week from your databank of expertise, keeps your profile dynamic, exciting and up to date.

## Contribute to groups

Most of the business networks have groups where your expertise will be greatly appreciated. By posting in these groups and sharing your knowledge, you will build your reputation both as an expert and as a contributor. This in turn will help build your contacts, as people will want to connect with you and in time to do business with you.

## Sharing knowledge

One of the strengths of social networking is the sharing of little tips on how to optimize your business with counterparts at other companies within the same industry. Are you worried about giving your game away? If you were at a conference and you were sitting down talking, those types of things would come up in a discussion group. Use your judgement when trying to decide whether something is too sensitive

56    to share, and remember you will benefit from this too. Seeking external help can sometimes be less risky than ploughing on in isolation.

## Moving to new locations

If you are relocating to a new geographical area, either at home or
abroad, tapping your network for contacts in that area or seeking out
new contacts there can be helpful in getting to know the place before
you arrive. Similarly, be generous and helpful to someone moving to
your city.

## Identifying experts

As well as your business profile offering an opportunity for you to be
found and identified as an expert in your field, your networks and
their contacts are a rich source of expertise for you – and not just in
terms of business advice or tips. Need a speaker on the aviation sector
in India? Need business analysis on a potential merger? Need an
opinion on a breaking story? You can find them all through your
networks.

# *Advantages for the self-employed (and the employed too!)*

Social networking is essential if you are
self-employed. The benefits can far out-
weigh the costs, and it can be both time and
money efficient in making connections for
your business.

## Saving time

Having emphasized that social networking is time consuming, it can save you time too. Time taken away from the business in going to networking events can be unproductive and disruptive. If you aren't an early morning person, breakfast meetings can be excruciating. Lunchtime meetings might be easier but disruptive to the working day, and evening meetings aren't always appropriate, particularly if you are a working mother. Conducting your networking online enables you to choose a time that fits in with your working day and when you are at your most sociable.

### Rookie Buster

Conducting your networking online enables you to choose a time that fits in with your working day and when you are at your most sociable.

## Making the best contacts

While your local networks are great for meeting people who are also self-employed, some of your best contacts might be in another town, city or country, and without the online connections you would not get to "meet" them. The advantage of social networks is that you can search on specific criteria and find the people who match.

## Networking in your field

Often it is useful to have peer contacts with whom you can share information and share work if you are overloaded (or whom you can help out if they are overloaded), and who can give you constructive feedback on your work. Sometimes it helps just to chew an idea over or bounce it around with them. Finding others in your area of expertise becomes easy in the social networking arena – check out general business networks, and the clubs within those networks, but also the specialist networks.

### Rookie Buster

The advantage of social networks is that you can search on specific criteria and find the people who match.

## Finding support

Working for yourself can be a lonely activity. The freedom of being able to work when you like can be hugely liberating, but the downside is that there are no water cooler moments when you share thoughts with colleagues. Having a network can create that water cooler for you – whether those online colleagues are industry peers, mentors, advisers or just friends with a shared interest with whom you can chat online over a coffee at break time. Knowing you are part of something, a bigger network of others just like you, can be tremendously comforting as well as useful for support, advice and just connecting with another human being.

### Rookie Buster

Knowing you are part of something, a bigger network of others just like you, can be tremendously comforting.

# Navigating the networks

There are new business networks springing up all the time on the internet. Some are international and some national or regional. Joining one of the larger international networks will help you find more local ones, and usually people within those local networks belong to several of them. Connecting with people from your own locality on these networks will lead you to the more active local business community groups in your area.

The following networks are examples of the larger business communities with international members. These aren't the only networks, but they are certainly a useful place to start for your business networking presence. You need to investigate several before you find the one that suits you best.

It is worth noting that most of these business networks have a basic free entry level, and paid-for subscriptions for higher levels of contact and functionality.

## www.LinkedIn.com

LinkedIn was conceived as a way for professionals to find, and be found by, former colleagues and potential new ones. The site puts the concept of six degrees of separation into action. You may not know a potential new recruit or partner directly; but with a large enough network, someone you know or someone they know (and so on) almost certainly does. The site now boasts 22 million users in 150 industries.

## www.ryze.com

With a claimed 500,000 members across 200 countries, Ryze helps people make connections to grow their business, build their career and life, find a job and make sales. Members get a free networking-oriented home page and can send messages to other members. They can also join special networks related to their industry, interests or location.

## www.XING.com

According to their website, over 6 million business professionals use German-owned company XING to do business and promote their career. The site is multi-lingual and also allows you to see how people are connected.

## www.plaxo.com

Plaxo started with a different kind of address book, one that leverages the power of the network effect to stay up to date. Currently they host address books for more than 40 million people.

Plaxo also now has "Pulse", which is intended to be a better way for you to stay in touch with the people you actually know and care about – your family, your real-world friends, and the people you know from business. Pulse is a dashboard for seeing what the people you know are creating and sharing all over the open web. You can hook your Pulse account up to all the places where you create or share information, such as your blog, Flickr, Twitter, and so on.

## www.ecademy.com

Ecademy is a smaller network, but it still has a hefty global reach, with members in around 200 countries. It is a friendly network and, unlike most others, its founders Thomas and Penny Power are still very much involved and very much at its forefront. There are also active offline Ecademy clubs in local countries and regions.

## www.perfectnetworker.com

Perfect Networker is a relative newcomer, but is building membership fast. Their mission is "to help you surround yourself with serious business professionals who are truly committed to establishing, strengthening and nurturing long term, mutually beneficial relationships with you, and to then provide you with the education and business tools to do that". The organization employs a formal programme of

instruction, included at no additional cost, through which members
are provided with tools and training to grow their businesses more
effectively.

## *Business netiquette*

The guidelines for social networking etiquette in Chapter 3 apply for
business networks too. However there are also some additional guidelines to observe here.

The biggest NO is mass broadcast, unsolicited or spam sales pitch-
ing. Just don't do it!

If you are on the receiving end, however, veteran networker Tom
"The Bookwright" Evans (www.thebookwright.com) suggests the
martial arts approach to deflecting it. Either send a direct sales pitch
back without acknowledging theirs, or, if you prefer a slighter softer
approach, respond with a "Not for me, thank you, but you might be
interested in my product/service [which you then pitch], or do you
know someone else who is?" They won't spam you again.

Some networks allow you to see your contacts' contacts. This can
be a source of profitable new connections, but do not pester second-
degree contacts incessantly. It can be counter-productive to approach
someone with whom you have only a tenuous link, and your own
direct contact won't be very happy about it. Better to ask them for an
introduction if possible.

Although there isn't a specific rule on this, if you are employed, you
do need to consider whether there is conflict of interest in publicly
networking or nurturing online relationships with employees at rival
companies.

Good networkers will go where the energy is, and they will not
force a relationship if there does not seem to be a spark there. If there
isn't the synergy between you, don't push it. It will only rebound on
you later – as in life, so online.

## Rookie Buster

Good networkers will go where the energy is, and they will not force a relationship if there does not seem to be a spark there.

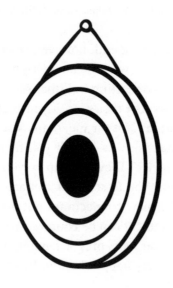

## Coach's notes

### 10 ways to get the best from your business network

1. **Know yourself and what you stand for.** What do you represent? When you leave a conversation or a message, do you leave something behind that reflects you? Something that others will remember you by?

2. **Network, don't sell.** Too many people see business networking as a selling opportunity. It isn't, and you won't get the best from your network if that is how you treat it. A business network is for business development, not for direct sales. Business development is sharing knowledge, resources and ideas. The networks out there are knowledge banks, not sales tools. Sure, plenty of referrals get passed and sales are made, but the intention is to share and build knowledge and contacts from which sales can later come. People come to trust you through your intentions, not your sales pitch.

3. **Create conversation.** Your network is not an audience to broadcast to; it's a place to create dialogue, conversation and connection. Making occasional announcements is fine, but avoid a daily newsletter. Personal contact with a personal message is much more effective and welcome.

4. **Have a purpose to the connection.** Do have some level of contact with a person before inviting them to connect with you. Some networks automatically connect you if you make contact and the recipient responds. When you make contact, make it meaningful, not just another scalp to add to your list. Read profiles carefully and find something in common that you can mention in your message. If someone has never heard of you they may wonder why you want to be in contact. Give them a reason and an intention for the connection.

5. **When you make a request, be clear about your intention.** Your contacts are generally happy to forward your requests if you approach them politely and are clear about your

purpose. If you are looking for particular connections, state clearly who, what and why.

6. **Express gratitude.** If someone has connected you or referred you, say thank you and reciprocate if you can. That could mean an offer to make a useful introduction; or an offer to help in some other way; or just a heartfelt thank-you for the introduction you seek. Giving a testimonial is a great way of saying thank you.

7. **Avoid the boilerplate text, if you can.** This is the standard text that is supplied for you to send when you invite friends and colleagues to connect to your network. It is so much nicer for the recipient to have a personal message saying why you thought of them and why you think they would benefit from being part of this network. Give them a reason to join.

8. **Be magnetic.** Put yourself out into the network by contributing and sharing. Share your knowledge and expertise, but also share a positive attitude and energy. Radiate happiness in being part of the network. That will start to draw others to you. We are all drawn to happy people.

9. **Be referable.** Make sure your profile clearly explains you and your product or service in a memorable way. If people don't understand what you do and how you bring value, they can't recommend you, however much they might like you. The art of networking is being talked about as much as being talked to, and your contacts won't talk about something they don't understand.

10. **Be reliable and trustworthy.** Always do what you say you are going to do, or give a good reason why you can't or haven't. People won't recommend or refer you if they can't be sure you'll deliver. Reputation takes time to build, but can be destroyed in seconds if you don't follow through on your promises.

**Go for it!** "The simple truth is that your reputation in the marketplace is dictated by how many people understand you, and what you do, and trust your abilities enough to recommend you to others with confidence. It's a closely coupled combination of factors – the number and quality of people you are directly connected to, the number and quality of people *they* are connected to and the degree to which your contacts are happy to refer you to someone else, because they feel comfortable that in promoting you, they will not jeopardize their own reputation." Rory Murray, Return on Relationships (www. returnonrelationships.net)

66 Notes

............................................................................
............................................................................
............................................................................
............................................................................
............................................................................
............................................................................
............................................................................
............................................................................
............................................................................
............................................................................
............................................................................
............................................................................
............................................................................
............................................................................
............................................................................
............................................................................
............................................................................
............................................................................
............................................................................
............................................................................
............................................................................
............................................................................
............................................................................
............................................................................
............................................................................
............................................................................
............................................................................
............................................................................
............................................................................
............................................................................
............................................................................

Notes

Online communities were the forerunner of social networks, though they are still very much alive and going strong. They include discussion groups, forums, message boards and chat rooms, all with a focus on collaboration, discussion and sharing of information, thoughts and opinions. Where they differ from networks is that the focus is on discussion, not on collecting contacts. Although most online communities have a brief profile page, members' profiles are peripheral to the discussions. In contrast, niche networks are much more profile driven and are about connecting with like-minded people. What online communities and niche networks have in common is that their focus is on one very specific topic and is not a general playground like FaceBook or MySpace. This chapter will give you an overview of these two types of communities, some tips on how they might fit into your networking strategy, and some guidance on whether and when to set up your own.

# CHAPTER 5

# Navigating your way though online communities and niche networks

## *Commonalities and differences*

### Profiles

Social networks use member profiles to represent and build member identity. These member home pages are at the very core of the network. You can build your identity through your profile, gather contacts and never participate in any groups or discussions. In online communities there is usually a brief profile page, which may include a picture, location, basic information and recent posts, but not much else. Often members of communities have an alias name and don't use their own; for example, HorseAddict or BigMan. Although the profile can add context to the community, it is not the main identifier of the user – their posts and contributions are.

# Collaboration

Online communities rely on collaboration and participation, otherwise the community dies. Members create relationships and their community identity through the information they post in the online discussions. The community could be just a handful of members, but still very active.

Networks rely on members joining, creating their profiles and inviting others to join. A member's identity can be created and built solely through the information on their profile and the connections they make. The network could be huge or small, with no collaboration beyond adding members. It can be very passive, with little discussion or sharing beyond the profile page. While that makes for a less interesting network, it nevertheless can survive and thrive.

## Explicit/implicit relationships

In traditional online communities, members' connections to particular discussion groups, forums or other members are implicit. They are not disclosed or made explicit to other members of the community. Members may have favourite members that they like to discuss with, but that information is not shared with the community either.

Social networks on the other hand enable members to show and share their explicit relationships and connections with other people. Members use their profile pages as rich representations of their preferences and interests, through the relationships they build and the connections they make.

## Formation of groups

New groups in online communities are generally a subset of an existing group, and are built within the specific structure and static hierarchy of the community. So in a discussion group about pets, you might end up with a forum on antisocial barking, but it will be a twig on the branch rather than the branch itself. For example, the branch might 71 work as follows: Pets – dogs – dog behaviour – antisocial behaviours – barking.

In social networks, new forums or groups can be created by individual members without being a subset of something else. In this way new branches grow all the time, and as popularity and membership of the group grow, they have an equal opportunity to gain visibility. So the topic of antisocial dog barking could be a thread within a discussion group on pets, but it could be a whole new discussion group of its own.

## Navigation

Traditional online communities use the discussions and forum posts and threads as the tools of navigation. So to get to the tips on controlling antisocial dog barking, you have to go through the pet forum and dig into it to find what you are looking for. In many ways        y o u need to know what you are looking for – or at least an area you are searching in – to find the information you want.

Social networking uses a quite different form of navigation, via people and their interests. You might visit your friend Jake's profile and see he is a member of the New Writers group, so you take a look at that group and find an interesting post from Rory about using blogs to promote your writing, so you go take a look at Rory's page and find he is an expert in social media marketing, which is exactly the kind of help you need to build your online presence. Rory has no other connection to Jake. In this way, seemingly random threads can actually lead you to just the information or people you need or want to connect with.

**Rookie Buster**

Seemingly random threads can actually lead you to just the information or people you need or want to connect with.

# Online communities as part of your social networking strategy

Online communities are useful places to join and frequent if you have a specific area of interest that you wish to know more about, share with other like-minded people, or gather information on; for example for market research. Clearly, if you are a pet food supplier, then listening in on and participating in the communities that are discussing their pets is a useful thing to do.

**Rookie Buster**

Online communities are useful places to join and frequent if you have a specific area of interest that you wish to know more about.

The main advantages in joining an online community for a business purpose are that it gives you the opportunity to hear what customers are really saying and thinking, and it gives you the opportunity to offer advice and help, thus drawing attention to you and your products or services. Overt selling is not appropriate, but if your product is the solution to the problem being talked about, then it is OK to say so and perhaps offer a free sample or a

discount to members of the forum. As with all "social" activity, you
have to earn your right to promote by being a valued participant first.

If you are thinking of setting up your own community (more of that later in the chapter), then researching other communities in the same topic area is a must, so that you can see how they work and what the popular discussion points are.

**Rookie Buster**

If you are thinking of setting up your own community, then researching other communities in the same topic area is a must.

Joining an online community to share in a specific common interest can also lead to other connections. For example, joining a community for dog lovers might lead you to other dog-related sites, which might lead you to a dog-walking group in your locality, where you meet someone who belongs to a useful business network that you subsequently join and that leads to connections you didn't even know existed.

While you should aim to have a strategy for every site you join, and maybe your primary networking focus is business, don't underestimate the power of those purely social connections and shared interest communities. They can be a rich source of contacts beyond the shared love of dogs.

## Niche networks as part of your social networking strategy

Niche networks are exploding across the internet, but have been around for several years, predating the big hitters like MySpace and Facebook. They just haven't had the media exposure that the

74  number-crunching general sites have achieved. When Ning (www.
ning.com) offered the technology to set up your own social network
for free, it opened the floodgates for thousands of sites to be created.
Prior to that, setting up a social network was a costly exercise and not
for the faint-hearted. There are many other companies who also offer
the technology and opportunity to set up your own network, but Ning
made it easy and cheap. Over 230,000 niche networks have been set up
on the Ning platform, and more get developed every day.

Membership of niche networks varies greatly, from a few hundred
to a few million. Some are invited membership only and closed to
public view, others are open to anyone with an interest in that topic.
And because there is a network for just about everything you could
possibly think of, from cars to comics, parenting to politics, intelligence to travel, IT to marketing, you should have no problem finding
one that fits.

The value of joining a niche network is obvious – it is a group of
like-minded people with a very specific focus. Therefore you are more
likely to build close relationships within a niche network than in a
generalist one, particularly in some of the smaller networks. Members
of niche networks view more pages, spend more time on the site and
come back more often. You are also more likely to find industry peers
or leading thinkers in niche networks and niche groups on the larger
business networks. Because you are more likely to build closer relationships with like-minded people in a niche, the opportunities for
developing business from the network become greater too.

**Rookie Buster**

You are more likely to build closer relationships with
like-minded people in a niche.

Many of the up-and-coming niche networks, particularly in the
business universe, focus very strongly on connection, conversation

and collaboration. They want active participants rather than passive
observers.

## Examples of niche networks

I have chosen three diverse niche networks as a flavour of what is out
there in the business sphere.

**Industry-focused: FashionNetworks (www.fashion-networks.com)**
An international business network specifically for the fashion industry, it calls itself the "leading online business networking platform
focused exclusively on the Fashion Value Chain". It aims to connect
the entire chain from fibre to textile, manufacturing to retail, providing a platform for fashion professionals – suppliers, retailers, manu-
facturers, sellers, buyers, designers – to share knowledge and
experience, keep up with current trends and industry developments,
locate business opportunities and seek out career moves. It is an open
network: anyone can join, and although you have to join to view
profile details, you can see who is there and view discussion threads
without joining.

**Philosophy-focused: Rebel Island (www.rebelisland.net)**
Rebel Island is a private international network that aims to connect
people "who live their lives by being purposeful, passionate and pro-
vocative in their work, lives and thinking. People who share the values
and visions of a new age for business and society and who want to
work with others to awaken the world to a new level of evolution." The
network is not open to all and you need to be invited or apply to join.

Founder Seán Weafer, self-proclaimed "rebel in a business suit", set
up the network to "collect people like me who take a different perspec-
tive on business; thought leaders and clients who share the values of
connection, collaboration, co-creation and community, and who want
to engage in dialogue with others who share their philosophies and
perspectives. By creating a social network, we get to synergize and
leverage many brains internationally."

A Rebel Island has also been created on Second Life, exclusively for members, where they will be able to create and participate in virtual meetings, conferences and seminars to share this leading-edge thinking.

**Collaboration-focused: Angels Den (www.angelsden.co.uk)**
Angels Den was set up by Scottish accountant Bill Morrow out of frustration at not being able to raise funding for his own business venture. He founded the network to make it much easier for entrepreneurs and financiers to connect with each other. "What it does is maximize the angels' minimal resource – time… they can log in and see the latest initiatives online. Entrepreneurs have low-cost access to so many more potential investors than they have ever had and valuable feedback that helps them hone their ideas."

The site offers tips and help to entrepreneurs and helps them develop business plans through a template that has been designed to get the information that angels want to see, in the way they want to see it. Entrepreneurs pay a fee to join.

# Creating your own – what you need to know

When you have gained some experience in this networking game, you might be tempted to start your own community or network.

## Online communities

Building an online community (which will usually be a part of your website) gives your visitors and customers the chance to interact with each other and feel a part of something. These connections will keep them coming back, and give them a reason to stay interested in your site. They will visit your site more often to participate. But if you create an area for your web community and no one comes, it does you no favours at all. You need to be sure that a community will work on your

website and that you have the time and inclination to put into building
it up before it can fly on its own. So you need to plan before you build.

- You need to find out if your customers are online already, where they are visiting currently, what groups they belong to and how willing they are to share information.
- You need administrators: people who are actually participating in the community from the "inside". It might be you or your employees who answer questions, participate in chat, or write the company blog. Once a community gets going, it can take a lot of time to keep active. If you can't keep up the level of attention, the participants will leave because they're feeling ignored or bored.
- You need to have a voice for the community that matches your audience: too formal for a casual crowd and you've lost them (and vice versa). And your team needs to know what they can and can't say online.
- It's not enough to just put up a forum and let people start posting. You need to start them off on interesting topics related to your business that they can be passionate about – and preferably positive topics, not whingeing about your service.

Think about what you're aiming for before building an online community. You may think it is just a matter of setting up a forum or a chat room and then sitting back and waiting for the people to come in, but there is a lot more to it.

You can create an online community in a variety of ways:

**Message boards and forums**
Most forum software allows people to browse through the postings before logging in, and once they feel comfortable they can set up their alias and submit their own posts.

**Web based chat rooms**
Chat rooms bring instant interactivity to a website. They also bring more anonymity than a message board. Your visitors can come into a chat room, give themselves any name they like and talk to other people with similar interests. Someone will act as moderator so you can have

78 hosted chats and control the room. Once you have a chat room, you can set up regular sessions or informal meetings, or just allow people to come and go as they please.

### Calendars
These can be as simple as lists of events, dates and times. They are an invaluable tool for building community, as they allow your visitors to find out what's happening. You can and should list events like your chat room schedule, guest authors, or forum topics to be discussed, as well as events of interest outside your site. If your visitors find that they can get valuable information from your calendar, they will come back to see what's happening.

### Niche networks
A niche network would normally be separate from your business website, not part of it. When you build an online community around your business or area of expertise, the focus is on the discussions rather than the members. Setting up a network is about connecting people with a common interest and enabling them to build relationships with one another and with you.

**Rookie Buster**

Setting up a network is about connecting people with a common interest and enabling them to build relationships with one another and with you.

There are a number of reasons why you might start a network of your own (this is not an exhaustive list!):
• To place yourself or your brand at the centre of this community, facilitating connections to raise your own profile and reputation – rather like hosting a table at a business dinner.

- To build your own connections and relationships within your niche area.
- For your own personal development and that of the others in your network.
- To enable like-minded people to connect.
- To gather thought leaders and "brains" together to exchange ideas and collaborate.
- To create dialogue and conversations around a specific topic.
- To bring people together who would find it hard to meet otherwise (such as entrepreneurs and business angels).

There are a number of platforms that enable you to build your own network. Ning seems the most popular, because it is a free service (though you can pay for a premium service if you want to have no ads or your own ads on your network) and anyone can use it to set up their network. You set up your network on Ning and your network members get a Ning ID, which they can also use to join any social network that is hosted on the Ning platform. The advantage for you is that you don't have to host your network on your own server; the disadvantage is that unless you spend money to create a custom front page to your Ning site, it will look rather similar to every other Ning site on the web.

To get the best from your niche network, you need to be clear about your ethos and purpose for the site, and you need to have a message behind it and a reason for people to want to join – something unique that you are offering them. The more exclusive it is, the more compelling it will be to join. Everyone likes to feel they are part of a private club.

You need to put time into building the network and inviting people to join. Eventually it will gather its own momentum, but until it does you have to actively work it to build it. There will always be "listeners" – those who join but don't participate. Encourage those who do engage and are active in the network. Social networks need to be constantly innovating, providing rich content and bringing members together if they are to be a key part of their members' lives.

80

**Rookie Buster**

Social networks need to be constantly innovating, providing rich content and bringing members together if they are to be a key part of their members' lives.

You will need to actively manage the growth and development of the network if it is to be successful. Your reputation is also at stake here, and you will be measured by your peers on how successful you are at attracting the "right" people in and keeping them. By the same token, when you achieve what you set out to do, your reputation will have a tremendous boost!

## Coach's notes

### How do I know if doing it myself is for me?

Six things to consider when deciding whether to build a network or just join a network.

**1. How much time can you devote to it?**

Setting the network up technically might be quick, but nurturing and growing it is not. Can you devote at least 10 hours per week initially to get it going and then consistently give 5–10 hours per week to keep tending it so it grows and gathers momentum?

**2. How interested are you?**

Are you passionate enough about the subject and the project to put the time in to populate the network with interesting people and content that will draw others in too? It isn't just a numbers game, it's a content game too. If there isn't enough happening on the site, then people will wander – or at least will become passive rather than active participants.

**3. Are you a natural connector?**

Do you really enjoy interacting with others, playing host and connecting up people and their interests? To run a successful network you have to be a good networker. You need to be persistent without being a pest. You need to be able to see connections where others might not. You must be able to build and follow up on relationships. You must welcome new people and help them settle in, not just leave them to flounder around in the dark. It's your party and you want everyone to stay and enjoy themselves.

**4. How well do you know your chosen topic?**

How easily can you create content to get and keep the ball rolling? Particularly in the early days you will have to actively stimulate discussions, write blog posts and keep the content fresh and up to date. Have you got enough knowledge of your niche to be able to do that easily and with little stress to you and your loved ones? Have you got other close colleagues who could share this burden with you?

**5. Are you in for the long haul or a quick hit?**

If you want a quick hit to raise your profile or build your connections, join a network, don't create one. Building a niche network is a long-term commitment (we're talking years) and you need to be prepared to go the distance. You might get others interested in taking it over or buying you out if there is enough value in the network, but to get it to that point you have to be prepared to give it whatever it takes, for however long it takes.

**6. Are you willing to invest in making it successful?**

While you can set up a niche network for free, you ultimately want it to stand out from the crowd of me-too networks – and so do your members. Are you able and willing to invest hard cash in it if and when necessary?

If you aren't answering a resounding yes to all of the above – don't do it.

**Go for it!** Do you come here often? You'll notice in any online community that there are participants and there are very active participants. The most active are the ones that other people want to be around, to know and to link to. They are the ones who will get the best return on their investment in time and energy; and the ones who will be doing the most business. Why? Because they are visible. They may not be the experts themselves, but they look as though they might be and they'll always know the person who is. The more targeted your niche – whether it's a network or a community – the more visible you can be.

*Notes*

*Notes*

Blogging has become the in-thing for building networks, communities, connections, reputation and profile. Everyone, from politicians to the average man in the street, is using it to express opinions and share information. Blogs have become almost more important than web-sites, and because readers can add their own comments, blogs start to become conversations within a network of interested people. They are much better than standard websites for search engine rankings because of their frequently updated and topical content, and because they are often linked to by other bloggers.

# CHAPTER 6

# Becoming a blogger

## *What is blogging?*

A blog is essentially a diary or journal, just one that you write on the internet rather than in a book. There are a number of free sites you can use to write your blog. Blogger (www.blogger.com) and Wordpress (www.wordpress.com) are the two most popular. There are also paid-for sites such as Typepad (www.typepad.com).

Your blog can be integrated into your website or it can exist as a separate domain. Whether you integrate or not depends on what your blog is for, and how it fits with your business. If you are employed, then you need to consider how your blog might reflect on or affect your position. Are you blogging for the company or for yourself?

**Rookie Buster**

Your blog can be integrated into your website or it can exist as a separate domain.

These are the things you need to consider in developing your blog.

## The personality of your blog

Blogs are not objective, nor should they be. Your blog is your biased opinion. It can be controversial, and you should certainly aim to stimulate debate and comment. Writing a blog is like writing a letter or diary. After a while the reader should be able to sense your values and interests; they should get a sense of who you are and not just what you do.

You can't remove the person or the personality from the blog. Your blog is an extension of your personality, a place to express your opinion and to build relationships by your reader getting to know you.

## Your voice

Your blog also needs to have a voice of its own – an author's voice; the voice of your personality. You should write to your reader just as you would speak to them. Your voice may be direct, informal, humorous, ironic, witty, natural, controversial, even irritating or cynical. You may create a personality and a voice especially for your blog. The purpose is to engage, inform and entertain, especially if you want to build a community of followers. Think of yourself as a newspaper columnist – they have a personality and a voice in their writing. You probably have columnists you love and those you hate. Either way you know their voice. Your blog is your voice on the internet.

**Rookie Buster**

The purpose is to engage, inform and entertain, especially if you want to build a community of followers.

# Making links

Blogging has been called the art of linking, and links to other context-specific material are a major part of most blogs. As blog readers we want links to other web pages that will be of interest. The web grows so rapidly we have no chance of keeping up, so we are starting to rely on our favourite blogs, links and feeds to bring us the information we seek rather than having to trawl endlessly through the internet to find it.

You therefore have an important role for your blog as the connector of information that is relevant and important to your reader. Networking is all about connecting, so links on your blog are an excellent way of connecting people to other people and to information.

**Rookie Buster**

Networking is all about connecting, so links on your blog are an excellent way of connecting people to other people and to information.

## Having conversations

It's unlikely that you are the only one on the internet talking about your subject. There are usually other bloggers who share your interests. You become a part of the conversation by linking to those blogs from posts of your own, stating your opinions and publishing related information or thoughts. If you do it well, they will link to you too, and this starts a kind of cyberspace conversation between blogs. It's not necessary to actively try to converse, but it is good when this happens because it helps to widen your network and build the relationships within it.

## 90  How much, how often?

Blogs are immediate, almost instantaneous. Blogs are at their best when you get the feeling that the blogger publishes as soon as he or she has something to say. It is better to post a little comment or thought every day rather than an essay once a month. Blogging should be fun for you, too, so don't make it an onerous task or you just won't do it. You are aiming to be a voice, a personality who people want to engage with. They need to have enough exposure to you to be able to engage and to look forward to hearing from you.

### Rookie Buster

Blogging should be fun for you, too, so don't make it an onerous task or you just won't do it.

If you have a lot to say, then say it, but beware of being verbose. Do you want to read a long, boring post that could have been written in half the words? No, of course not! Short, sharp, relevant and to the point; little and often is best.

## Feeds

Most blogs are published both on websites and as so-called feeds. Regular readers of your blog will probably have it bookmarked and they may subscribe to a news feed that allows the new content of your blog to be "fed" to the reader without them having to visit your site.

## When to integrate with your own website 91

Is your strategy to build a network to develop your business, or to develop your personal profile? What voice and personality are you planning for your blog? Does this fit the values and ethos of your business, or will you feel restricted in your opinions if you integrate your blog into your website? If the blog is related more to gaining awareness and networking for your business, then integrate it; if it is more for developing your personal connections and your personal profile, then keep it separate.

It is worthwhile starting out with a separate personal blog while you get some blogging experience before taking it to the next level and blogging to raise awareness of your expertise and your business.

# *The value of a personal blog*

### Learn the skills of blogging and find out what works for you

If you haven't blogged before, then a personal blog can be a good training ground and useful in helping you to get to know the tools, techniques and art and craft of blogging. It is easy once you get the hang of

it, and as when learning anything new, the more you do it the easier it gets. Once you have mastered the basics, then you can experiment with other blog tools and platforms that might better suit your networking and profile building needs.

## 92 Work out how much time you have

Many new entrepreneurial bloggers underestimate the amount of time
and energy that building a successful blog can take. Starting out with
a personal blog gives you a taste of what is involved and how much
time you can (and want to) devote to it.

## Work out if you can sustain blogging for the long term

Personal blogs are a good way to get a feel for whether blogging is actually for you. While blogging is certainly recommended, blogs are not
for everyone. Better not to blog at all than do it half-heartedly. It will
show in the personality and voice of your blog and will defeat the
object of having one. Writing a personal blog just about the things that
you love gives you a realistic feel for whether you actually enjoy it. You
also begin to develop your own "rhythm" of blogging, which will help
with your business blog and networking activity.

### Rookie Buster

While blogging is certainly recommended, blogs are
not for everyone. Better not to blog at all than do it half-
heartedly.

## Find your voice

Sometimes, particularly if you don't write regularly, it takes a while to
find your voice and your style. It's safer to experiment and play with
this on a personal "play" blog before you start your business or "expert"
blog, where your reputation will be at stake. You can try different
voices, different personalities and different topics, and ask trusted

friends and colleagues to give you feedback. When you are happy with your voice and the topics that you can talk on with ease and authority, then go for it!

## Find your readership

Another benefit of blogging on a more personal level is that over time you begin to connect with more and more people. As you blog on topics that appeal to others, you'll find some people will keep coming back for more. When you're ready to launch your "expert" blog you are able to leverage some of your personal blog's traffic and will start with a more established readership.

**Rookie Buster**

As you blog on topics that appeal to others, you'll find some people will keep coming back for more.

## Get to grips with blogging "culture" and rules

There is an unspoken etiquette around blogging. Many of the rules and customs are just common sense, but for clarity here are the main things you need to be aware of and adhere to:

- Only publish as fact those things that you know or believe to be true. If in doubt, don't publish it, or state clearly that it is speculation or rumour only, and not fact.
- If material you are referring to or discussing in your post exists online, link to it as well as referencing it. It is these links to source material that create the collective network of information and knowledge. And of course if someone was referring to you in their writing, you'd want them to link to you too.
- Write your posts with integrity and intent. Add to posts if you

have further information or comment, but don't rewrite, change or delete posts once published, because if someone links to your post and then it disappears or changes, it breaks the connections and conversation. It's also very irritating when you want to read a link only to find it's no longer there.

- Correct your mistakes, but (as in the previous point) don't delete them. If you find that you have linked to a story that was untrue, make a note of it and if possible link to a more accurate one. If you discover that your own statement proves to be inaccurate, make a correction on your blog with the accurate information. Ideally, add a note to your original post too, as search engines will pull up entries without regard to when they were posted; once an entry exists in your archives, it may continue to spread the inaccuracy even if you corrected the information a few days later.

- Disclose any conflict of interest. Be transparent. If you are recommending a product, service or company because you stand to benefit, then say so. A brief reference to your interest is fine.

- If you are quoting or linking to a strongly biased source, mention that bias in your post so that readers have the information they need to evaluate the merits of the source for themselves, and can then make their own minds up on the subject.

The best rule to follow when blogging, in order to avoid any misunderstandings, is: *if in doubt, leave it out!*

# The value of a business-related blog

## Be the expert

Blogging is a good way to position yourself and your company as the expert or the thought leader in your industry. If you share your knowledge and expertise through regularly posting on topics you know are pertinent in your industry, then you will become known as the person who knows. This builds your reputation and places you first in mind when someone is looking for your expertise.

## Customer relationships 95

In a forum where your main objective is not to sell, you'll have a more personal relationship with your customers. Blogs are a fast way to join the customers' discussions, provide tips and insights or receive feedback.

### Rookie Buster

Blogs are a fast way to join the customers' discussions, provide tips and insights or receive feedback.

## Media relations

Your blog is PR for you and your business. All too often, press releases end up in the bin without being read, but journalists are always looking for topical opinion. If your blog becomes popular and provokes frequent comment or debate, and is well linked to others, you will generate media interest. You become their expert on your subject and you will be the one they turn to first for comment on that subject.

## Collaboration, and gathering and managing knowledge

Sharing knowledge and opinion through your blog and through collaborative conversations with other bloggers is a good way of developing relationships and gathering knowledge for yourself. Your network is a rich source of information which you can tap into, and connect others to, through your blog.

If you are working within a project team, a blog

96 can also be used as a workspace where team members keep each other updated and share information and knowledge without wasting time writing reports or searching their email inbox. Such blogs can be made private so that only the authors or members can view them.

## Attracting good people

If you establish yourself and your company as the experts in your industry, people will pay attention. They'll read and discuss what you have to say. It's quite likely they will see you as an attractive employer, and the better candidates will be keen to join you.

## Informal market research

When you want some feedback, but can't afford or don't want to conduct formal research, your blog is a good way of getting informal comment. It can provide you with a measure

of value. Do you have a new or improved product or service you want to test? Publish the idea and see if it generates interest. Does anyone link to you? What do they say? Offer a free trial to your network in return for feedback and comment.

## Rank high in search engines

Google and other search engines reward sites that are updated often, link to other sites and, most importantly, have many inbound links. A blog on your website can boost your rankings. This can help build your network, as it is easier for people to find you when you appear on the first page of an internet search. Putting your blog and website link on your profile for any networks you belong to and a link to the networks from the blog also helps your ranking and your ability to be found.

**Rookie Buster**

A blog on your website can boost your rankings. This can help build your network, as it is easier for people to find you when you appear on the first page of an internet search.

## Keep a historical record of your expertise

Your blog posts form a record that will become increasingly valuable over time. Because blog archives are searchable, downloadable, and stored within the blog, you can use them as a knowledge base and showcase for your expertise. Contacts can be directed to past posts for information.

## Additional etiquette for business blogging

- Make it clear that the views expressed in the blog do not necessarily represent the views of your employer or your company.
- Respect the company's confidentiality.
- Be respectful to the company, other employees, customers, partners and competitors. Give a balanced view or make it very clear that your post is just your opinion.
- Be aware of the impact your posts could have on others and on your position or reputation.
- Observe company requests that certain topics are not discussed for confidentiality or legal compliance reasons.

98
- Ensure that your blogging activity does not interfere with your work commitments.
- Be prepared to delete inappropriate comments, spam or off-topic material.
- Don't discuss private issues relating to colleagues or the company on your blog.

**Top tips for your best blog**

1. **Set your purpose.** Decide what you want to accomplish with your blog and focus your writing around that. Are you blogging to learn the art of doing it? Are you blogging to find your voice? Are you blogging to share information and thoughts on a particular interest? Or are you blogging to build your profile and your following as an expert on a particular subject area? Clarity of purpose is key to writing your best blog.

2. **Know your audience.** Decide who you are writing for and who you want to attract to your blog. How would you address these people if you met them face to face? This will determine your appropriate tone of voice and your personality in this context.

3. **Be passionate about your subject.** Write about what you love, and write from the heart. If you haven't got a passion for your subject, no one will engage with your blog. Your interest must shine through. A blog is the place for controversy, strong opinion, debate and discussion. Use your love of your subject to ignite the passion of others for it too.

4. **Be vulnerable and approachable.** If your readers think you just know it all and are invincible, they'll be too scared to engage. Be open to (even invite) questions, comments and criticism. Don't be afraid to admit that while you know a great deal about the subject, you are still learning too. It makes you human and real. Blogging is about engaging with real people.

5. **Give good quality.** When you write, give the best quality information you can and link to others who give good quality too. That way your readers will keep coming back for more and you will gain their trust and be seen as a credible source.

Then you will encourage inbound links and your connections will grow (not to mention your search engine rankings).

6. **Use key words.** If there are specific key words that readers are likely to search on to find information on your subject, try to use them in your writing. Don't overdo it, though – your posts still need to be readable! The use of key words will help the search engines to find your blog ahead of another one on a similar topic.

7. **Post frequently.** Little and often (several times a week) is the key. Readers will keep coming back if there is something new on a regular basis. They'll lose interest if there isn't.

8. **Link, link, link!** Link to your sources, link to other blogs and link to websites. When you are actively linking to others, they will feel more inclined to link to you. When you link to a news story, an essay, a government document, a speech, or another blogger's entry, you allow your readers access to your sources so that they can make informed judgements. Your readers may enjoy being introduced to the blogs and websites that you most enjoy reading and that are of interest to you. Generously linking to other blogs grows the network of information sharing and social alliances for all.

9. **Be patient.** Your popularity won't explode overnight. It may take months or even years for your blog to grow its audience to its full potential. It may never have more than a few hundred regular readers, but those who come regularly will be those who are most interested in what you have to say, and they will be your advocates and referrers. They are worth their weight in gold.

10. **If it's a drag, you won't keep it up.** Make sure it is fun for you too. Even the most professional of blogs can have some humour and light-heartedness. Dare to experiment. You'll have more fun and so will your readers.

**Go for it!** Blogging can be a profound experience. Just the act of finding something in your everyday world to talk about makes you notice more clearly what is going around you. You might reflect on a book you are reading, the vastness of the sky on a day trip out of the city, a flower you noticed in a crack in a wall next to the bus stop, behaviours of people around you as they go about their business. When others read your reflections they start to take more notice too. As they follow the links from your blog to others they may form new opinions, change their views or learn something new. Through your blog, you won't just connect with other people and extend your network; you'll also affect their lives in ways you might never have imagined.

Notes

Notes

If you are looking to build and promote your brand, your personal profile in your industry and your reputation, social networking is the best and fastest way of reaching the widest audience. Whether you are looking for progression up the career ladder or for getting your name "out there" as the expert in your field, or for promoting your books or your business, your online presence is crucially important these days. This chapter will guide you through the use of social media to get yourself known.

# CHAPTER 7

# Personal branding and reputation, and building your career

## *Developing your online presence*

### Recognition and visibility

To develop your personal brand online you need to be highly visible in a number of different channels. The more people who connect your online profile to your existing brand or website the better. This is why it is so important that your visibility and profile on all the sites you frequent is consistent, and that they are linked. You may show different aspects of your life and personality, but they should present a coherent whole image. Your profile is crucial to building your personal brand, and the Coach's Notes at the end of this chapter focus entirely on how to create that killer profile.

**Rookie Buster**

To develop your personal brand online you need to be highly visible in a number of different channels.

106 The other elements that will make up your online brand are your website, your blog, links to you and from you via social bookmarking, your participation in discussions and groups, and articles that you write which can be found online. Visibility is familiarity or brand recognition. You not only want people to see your profile, but you want them to know and recognize it instantly. Wider visibility will also give you greater opportunities for networking as well as being known. Your visibility will also depend on your level of participation. You don't always have to be generating new content of your own; you can write just short references to the articles or sites of others who are writing in your area of expertise. You can be an expert at knowing the juiciest bits to pass on to save your readers time and energy in sorting through the mass of information available. If you aren't confident in your own writing, being a gateway and guide for others by frequent quoting and linking to articles and sites of interest can still be a good way to quickly build your online presence.

## Be an active participant with a continuous presence

Attention and influence accumulate with time and continuous presence. You need to maintain a continuous presence from the start. If you can't sustain regular posting, submitting, updating and participating, then consider whether building an online presence is for you. I've mentioned "little and often" in several chapters already, and that really is the key to building your reputation and personal brand. Better to do a regular weekly update or post than have a huge flurry of activity for two weeks and then nothing for a month.

The more active you are online, the more likely you are to build a strong reputation. The amount of time you spend on developing your presence is directly proportionate to the growth of your brand's online attraction. It needs to become a habit rather than a chore. The initial stage of building a profile will always require an investment of your time, though it gets easier over time because established brands tend to spread themselves, and your readers/connections will become your advocates and supporters, so spreading the word for you.

**Rookie Buster**

The more active you are online, the more likely you are to build a strong reputation.

## It's good to talk

Conversation is an integral part of building relationships, and it's a good way to make new friends or acquaintances who may be of mutual benefit in the future. Creating and encouraging dialogue and feedback is important to building your personal brand. People respond better to being talked *with* rather than talked *at*. The age of personal PR by giving out a one-way message is over. Always be open to communication. Ask for and listen to feedback. Use social networks as an opportunity to learn. Experts need the grapevine too.

Even as an expert, you can't know everything about your subject. Creating dialogue with other leading thinkers in your field is good, as it boosts your reputation and projects an image of being approachable and open. Sometimes being an expert is more about knowing the questions to ask than having all the answers yourself. Get good at and comfortable with asking questions of others in your field. Many people need those answers, but might not know the right question to ask.

108

**Rookie Buster**

Sometimes being an expert is more about knowing the questions to ask than having all the answers yourself.

## Put the community first

This may seem an odd thought, given that we are talking about building personal brands and reputation. However, your reputation doesn't just rest on what you know, or even who you know; it is also influenced by how you work your network and how you support the communities you inhabit.

Help new users find their way around the communities you belong to, and give them the benefit of your social networking experience as well as your knowledge of your subject area. Be an advocate of others and keep the referrals or introductions flowing. Offer constructive criticisms of the websites you use and help other users to get heard. Promote the profiles or stories of other users, where they deserve to be promoted.

This allows you to develop credibility, builds your overall reputation and gives you points for providing value to your network or community.

## Provide value, gain trust and attention

Value leads to the development of trust. To build a successful brand through social media, you should first earn trust by providing value through your participation.

### Rookie Buster

To build a successful brand through social media, you should first earn trust by providing value through your participation.

In Chapter 9 we'll look at social bookmarking in depth, and how to use social bookmarks to add value and complement your social networking and profile building activity. One area where you can add real value to your network and community is to use social bookmarking to submit stories from other sites and to direct traffic to them. Why would you do that? To associate your profile on these sites with being a giver of excellent value. If you submit only your own articles and your own websites, you'll build a reputation, but not the one you want. Be selfless. Ivan Misner, founder of Business Networks International, coined the phrase "Givers gain." That is definitely the case in using social media.

If you focus on providing value, other users will trust and follow you or your site more closely. You gain attention and your brand grows, which often leads to greater benefits in the future in terms of increased traffic, reputation or connections. Focus on giving rather than extracting benefit, and ultimately you'll get greater benefit in the long run.

## Integrity and ethics

Reputation is built slowly and can be lost in a flash, so you want to make sure that you're developing a legitimate social media presence, because the more successful you are at gaining visibility, the more people are keeping their eye on you. Check out each site's terms of use, and don't violate them. Make sure the people and stories you link to are legitimate, and if you discover they aren't, then do something about it – amend or remove your link and put a footnote as to why, or email the site administrators and ask them to do so.

110   You can experiment, but make sure that what is visible to your audience is legitimate. It only takes a few people and a few words to damage your reputation and all your hard work.

Apart from self-preservation, ethics can also improve the reputation of your brand. Be known for your integrity, honesty and trustworthiness. This is especially important for new brands entering the world of social networking, since they have no previous clout to leverage.

**Rookie Buster**

Be known for your integrity, honesty and trustworthiness.

## Case study: Tom "The Bookwright" Evans

Tom Evans is a good example of building your personal brand using social media. For starters, Tom has incorporated his brand into his name for his online presence. It's pretty clear Tom's brand is to do with writing books. He is very knowledgeable and experienced in social networking, but he isn't out there with a profile in every port. Tom's profile building activity is achievable by anyone, and is based on a consistent and steady presence in selected areas which he can leverage most successfully.

Tom has a primary business profile on Ecademy (www.ecademy.com), where he has amassed 1,787 connections over six years. Right up front on his profile he states who he is and what he does: "I am an author, business catalyst, poet and bookwright. My speciality is teaching authors and businesses where ideas actually come from and how to excel by tapping into inspiration on demand."

Tom also leads thirteen clubs on Ecademy including a club for writers wanting help with writing their books (his specialist subject) and a club for people wanting to gain more from their online networking (an area of solid experience but not where he is building his business). He actively participates in a number of others, giving value from his knowledge and his experiences.

Tom has an active blog (www.thebookwright.com), on which you can sign up for a regular newsletter. This helps Tom build a following and a database of interested readers. Tom's blog is also fed to his Ecademy profile.

You can follow Tom on Twitter, view his photos on Flickr and see what articles he recommends on StumbleUpon. You'll also find him on www.naymz.com, www.icontactcommunity.com, www.spock.com and www.linkedin.com, among others. He is just starting to develop his own social network in the book publishing field.

Tom's advice is: "The first key to making networking work for you is to notice serendipity and, when you do, to act on it. For example, when more than two people tell me to connect with someone, or for that matter to read a book, I make sure it's high on my to-do list. The second key is to make advocacy work for you. Even if you have a wide portfolio and range of skills, focus on the one thing you do best that is also the most memorable to drop into a conversation. For me, everyone I meet now gets a bookmark with The Bookwright logo on one side and a list of services on the other."

Take a leaf from Tom's book: find something that makes you memorable in all that you do, something that makes it easy for others to remember you from the crowd of people they network with. If you are first in their mind in your field, you will be the first one they refer.

### Rookie Buster

Find something that makes you memorable in all that you do, something that makes it easy for others to remember you from the crowd of people they network with.

# *Social networking for personal PR*

One of the biggest misconceptions about PR is that journalists are just sitting waiting for the thousands of press releases they receive every day to land in their inbox. They aren't. They really don't care if you have launched a new book, a new widget or a new service. What they care about is a good story. Why did you write the book, design the widget or know that the new service was needed? They want the human story behind it. So they scan the headlines of those press releases and repeatedly hit delete. While they are deleting endless news releases that have no real or apparent story, they are also surfing the internet to find out more about the odd one that caught their eye, or the story that they picked up through their online or offline connections. In journalism as in everything else, who you know and who knows you are key.

Therefore your social networking has two functions in PR terms to build your profile:

1. To be a source of good stories – including having good stories of your own.
2. To be a source of information that helps journalists write their piece.

## Being a story

When you are writing a post or an article, or contributing to a discussion, keep in mind the story you are telling – who, what, where, why and when; the "why" being the most important element. Think about the purpose of your piece; are you educating, entertaining or informing? Breaking it down into "10 steps to", "7 secrets of", and so on, helps both the reader and the journalist, particularly online, where long reams of unbroken text can be unreadable. Lists can also help you organize your thoughts.

## Pay attention to top 10 search results about you and your industry/area of expertise

On a daily basis, Google your area of interest: what is hot news that you can comment on? Who is writing on the subject and who is being written about – can you add something to their story by either commenting on it or writing your own post and linking to it? This adds to your visibility, but also puts your name alongside the regular writers so that when journalists do a search around that topic, your name should come up too.

## Be findable

Make sure you can be found by the search engines – blogs are good for this because they are frequently updated content that search engines like. If you need to take advice or ask for assistance on optimizing your presence on the web, do so. (There are useful tips about this in *Low-Budget Marketing for Rookies*.) Social bookmarking will also help – more about that in Chapter 9.

## Be accurate

Make sure that anything you report is accurate. Journalists check their facts too – if yours aren't right, they won't trust you as a source.

## Link and be linked

Wherever you write, include links to industry-related research or content that supports your story. The more help you can give a journalist searching for information on your topic the better. Again this will build their trust and your credibility. If you always provide plenty of back-up research and information to save them trawling the internet for it, they'll keep coming back to you.

114

**Rookie Buster**

Wherever you write, include links to industry-related research or content that supports your story.

## Propagate your contributions

To really build your online presence, you need the help of others to spread the word. Who in your network is willing to quote you, link to you and talk about you to others in their networks? This is where your relationship building comes in, and why it takes time. Forming a little syndicate with a few select and good contacts who operate in similar or complementary areas, and who also want to build their profiles, can be mutually beneficial for all. If you link to each other on your blogs (even if it is just on the blog roll – the list of other blogs you read) and in your posts, refer to each other's writing, articles and discussion posts (where appropriate), and bookmark each other's pages using one or more of the social news sites such as StumbleUpon or Delicious, it will help your visibility and help promote your name.

**Rookie Buster**

To really build your online presence, you need the help of others to spread the word.

## Make it bite-sized

If you have good stuff to share, share it in small bits, and give each of those bits their own permalink (a unique url for that post). Perhaps you have a super report chock full of data and exclusive to you that would really position you as a thought leader. Posting the entire

document only as one pdf limits your readership and interest levels. By
all means make the pdf accessible for those that want to read the whole
thing, but pull out each nugget or insight and write a separate post for
each, complete with links to the other posts and to the full pdf. Each
nugget can then be discussed on its own merits, others can link to that
post from their own sites, and the ensuing conversations, comments
and trackbacks can boost your visibility, your readership and your
search engine rankings.

## Follow the Twitter

To keep up to date with what the leading writers (both journalists and
experts) are up to, you need to subscribe to their Twitter feed and
follow their blog. This gives you the opportunity to build a relationship
with them by responding to their posts and their "tweets". A well-
aimed compliment and comment with a reference or trackback to
your own site or profile will do you no harm. However, do not stalk
them or bombard them with irrelevant messages! Think about how
you can *give* value to *them* first; the value to you comes from that later.

# *Using social networking for career development*

All of the above tips on building your online presence and personal PR
are relevant for career development too. If you stand out from the
crowd as being knowledgeable in your field and a good networker or
connector, you will get noticed by potential employers. These days, it
is likely that employers will do an internet search on you, so it's advisable to control what is said about you, and what you say, on the
internet!

**Rookie Buster**

It is likely that employers will do an internet search on you, so it's advisable to control what is said about you, and what you say, on the internet!

## Managing your online presence

It is crucial that you manage your online presence, and keep anything that would not be conducive to your career development either off the internet, or confined to your private friends network. We all do mad, bad and crazy things, and life would be tedious if we didn't, but you don't want the evidence of yours splashing across your accessible profiles. And ask your friends not to flaunt those pictures or stories either if you really want to maintain an online presence to build your career. No one expects you to be squeaky clean, but just be mindful of what image you are putting across.

Similarly, if you are blogging, be careful that what you blog about isn't going to incur the wrath of your company or the disdain of your peers. You can be critical, but always be constructive – and bad language is a definite NO.

## Networking for the future

If you know what career path you plan to take and the companies you'd like to work for, actively networking with employees of those companies can be useful. Just be mindful of talking about issues or information from your own company that could create a conflict of interest or give away trade secrets to your new contacts. Joining groups where your future colleagues or employers congregate can be helpful for getting yourself noticed or for listening in on their online conversations and gleaning knowledge about them and the company. You could also target specific people who might influence your career

progression, creating passive relationships around shared interests    117
and knowledge.

## Keep your CV online and up to date

Business focused networks like LinkedIn and Xing actively encourage
uploading your full CV on to your profile and connecting for career
purposes. Make sure you keep the CV up to date and include links to
your blog (if it is related to your career or expertise) and to other networks you belong to that are relevant.

## Ask questions

Make use of discussion boards, forums and specific Q & A areas to ask
questions relating to your industry or desired career. You can also ask
for specific help on your career path, career planning or career management. In these environments people are very willing to offer their
advice or assistance.

### Create your killer profile

Your profile is the most important element of your strategy, not least because it will reveal that strategy (or lack of it) to your connections. Remember: *you are your brand.* Here are seven tips to help you create that killer profile!

1. Google your own name and find out what is already being said about you on the web. Aim for consistency in your online image and try to have the same overall message whatever site you are found on. Think of your web presence as your overall profile and the different places where you are found as being complementary (and not conflicting) parts of it. You may focus more on social activities in one place and business in another, but the overall impact should be of a whole person, not fragmented parts.

2. It's often more important to be found than to find, and when people do find you, they need to find up-to-date information. The internet is one massive archive. Things that you were involved in years ago, websites on which you were mentioned, blogs you might have commented on or posted will stay there for ever. So make sure that somewhere on the web is the most recent information that you want people to know about. Take the time to make sure your profile is complete, regularly updated and reflects who you are and what you are currently doing. Include the keywords that somebody looking for you might use when searching.

3. Make sure your profile is in your voice; talk in the first person about yourself. Include something of who you are (your beliefs, your values, your thoughts on life). If you find that hard, ask a good friend how they would describe you to someone else. Include what you do (your work activity and your interests). Include specialist interests and specialist expertise (display

your flame!). Use the conventional words and phrases of your industry or interest; people will search on these.

5. On some sites, such as LinkedIn, everywhere you worked is an opportunity to reconnect with old friends and colleagues, so if appropriate add all your positions. Add depth to your positions too. If part of your profile is a résumé (particularly on some business or job-related sites), talk about what you have accomplished.

6. Add website links, activities, interests and awards. This is appropriate and acceptable self-promotion. People actually want this information on your profile (but not in messages and posts), so take advantage of it.

7. Talk about your networking needs. What is your purpose for being there? Who do you want to connect with and why? What can you offer or contribute? This is a good place to ask specifically for connections that can help you with your "wax" – the things you don't like doing or need help with, or advice about. Networkers are generous; we want to help and contribute, that's why we are all doing it.

**Go for it!** Until the advent of online social networks, building a personal brand and reputation was a long and expensive affair, usually entailing the hire of a good PR agent. Now the tools and the knowledge are available to drive your personal brand to the forefront. It's no longer about who has the most money to throw at their marketing and brand building: it's now about who has the most effective network, the most visible online presence and the capability to leverage both. It can cost next to nothing in hard cash, but the value is priceless!

Whether it's announcing your new ebook to your Facebook friends, surfing user groups to find out what is hot and happening, or testing out a new idea with a select group of trusted colleagues in your network, social networking is a tremendous opportunity for market research and for getting the word out. This chapter looks at some of the ways that you can use social networks to elegantly market your company and you.

# CHAPTER 8

# Marketing yourself and your business through social networking

## *Market research*

Traditional offline market research tends to use questionnaires and focus groups to canvass opinion. The flaw in traditional research is that opinion is just that – someone's thoughts on the matter, but not necessarily their motivation to buy. Many products have failed at the checkout because, while opinion showed the product was great, the pull to buy wasn't strong enough. So how can social networking help you avoid that mistake?

People are much more candid in their thoughts and feelings on their blogs and in community groups and discussions than they are in focus groups and surveys, where they tend to give what they think is the "right" or acceptable answer. Participating in the communities frequented by your desired audiences and reading the blogs of those participants can give you great information about the potential market for your product or service.

124

**Rookie Buster**

People are much more candid in their thoughts and feelings on their blogs and in community groups and discussions than they are in focus groups and surveys.

## Participate in communities

Participating in communities will also help you find out what the market need and desire is in your area of expertise. Maybe you were thinking of creating a particular product; but your community may be expressing a need for something different, in which case you can amend your offering before you get too far down the line with it, or throw it out altogether before you spend precious time and money on something which won't sell in the quantity you need it to.

## Follow blogs

Following discussions and blogs also helps you establish market or industry trends and find out who the current thought leaders are in your sector. If you know who the "names" in your sector are, Google them and find out what they are writing, where they are quoted and linked to, etc. If you don't know who they are, Google your sector and find out. Because these people will be building their own online profiles, they will be blogging and networking too. This gives you the opportunity to contact them via networking, to comment on their blogs, and to quote them on your blog. This gets you on to their radar and starts to position you alongside them in the eyes of others who are also researching.

# Follow Twitter

Twitter is a micro-publishing tool (a mini blog), which allows you to publish short messages of up to 140 characters through instant messaging, mobile phone texts or the internet. Twitter gives you an abridged version of opinions, events, news, ideas and feedback. It is structured so you can easily follow thousands of users and listen in on and enter into conversations among multiple users at any point. For market research purposes it can be a good tracking device for listening in on conversations about brands, products or services of specific interest to you. You can also use it to put out requests for feedback.

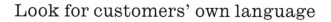

## Look for customers' own language

An area of market research which is starting to gain greater prominence and importance is that of finding out your customer's language – in other words, the exact words your customer uses to describe their experience of buying and using your or a competitor's product. You can only influence the behaviour of your customers by speaking to them in their own language. And this means using the exact words they use in a specific context, and conveying what is important to *them*. Taking the customer's words and then putting your own slant on them just does not work.

Remember New Coke? A classic mistake made by a classic brand. Taste tests indicated that the new formula was a winner – but the marketers underestimated the huge sentimental attachment to the original; the mere idea of something "new" caused outrage among customers, and New Coke was pulled pretty rapidly when it bombed at the checkout. If the marketers at Coca Cola had instead reassured customers that the new product was a little improvement but still just like the Coke they knew and loved, the outcome might have been different.

The thought leaders in this field of customer language are Diana

Tunney (www.thebestblog.info) and Shelle Rose Charvet (www.successstrategies.com). Di Tunney talks on her blog of how surfing the blogs and communities of your potential or actual customers can give you a good insight into the language they use and how they describe their experiences of your, or similar, products and services. Customers will talk about what is important to them, what annoys them, and what they love about it. Pick up on those keywords and you are halfway to marketing heaven. You'll also be stealing a march on most other marketers (even, or especially, big brands) who still see social media as computer-to-human interaction rather than member-to-member.

## Polls and surveys

Many sites also offer polls and surveys, or the opportunity to add surveys on to the profile. These can be a good way of gathering quantitative responses to multiple-choice questions. Be aware of the limitations of these polls, though, in terms of data you can work with. You can't always control who is responding, and they may not be in your target audience.

The real value of the insights you will glean from using social networks and social media for research is in the dialogue that is buzzing around the internet every day. Customers value the feedback and thoughts of other customers far more than they value your marketing speak or sales pitch. Social media empowers anyone to publish their voice and to be easily heard, which means you can easily read what they are saying. While negative customer feedback can be a disruption, it's also an opportunity – potentially an opportunity to fill the gap in that dissatisfaction.

**Rookie Buster**

Customers value the feedback and thoughts of other customers far more than they value your marketing speak or sales pitch.

One final point: if you are researching via blog posts remember to    127
read all the comments too. The best nuggets of information are sometimes in the comments, not the main post.

# Using your network to market your brand

The right approach to marketing has to start with a deep understanding of what your customers want – their needs and desires. So any
marketing strategy initiated through your networks assumes that you
know your customers, you know what they want, and your products
and services have been developed to fulfil their needs and desires.
Understanding your customers' behaviour is essential – what do they
actually say and do in the buying process? If you
haven't gathered that data, do so before trying
to promote your brand through social
networking.

The next piece of the puzzle is to know
your story or brand positioning. Is your
product faster, newer, better, cheaper?
Are you at the cutting edge with something new and exciting? Or are you sup-
plying something tried, tested and
trusted? Think of a word: safety, for
example. Which brands immediately
come to mind? As humans all we work
with is stories. What is your story? What
words are, or do you want to be, synonymous
with your brand?

Your products and services are the phys-
ical manifestations of your story or brand. How do
your products fulfil the story you want to tell? Have you got testimonials and quotes from customers or advocates that demonstrate the
effectiveness of your products or service?

So assuming you have this information, how can you use social

128 networking to market and promote you, your brand and your products/services?

Remember: the whole point of social networking is interaction and connection; dialogue, not monologue. Talking *at* your connections and customers is pointless; always aim to talk *with* them. The intention is to stimulate and gather a tribe of people talking about you and with you, not to be the lone voice in an uninterested crowd.

## Rookie Buster

The intention is to stimulate and gather a tribe of people talking about you and with you, not to be the lone voice in an uninterested crowd.

Marketing is all about building long-term relationships that create trust and loyalty, which in turn create revenue and greater profit. Social/business networking is about that too. Just as you need to consider who you want to attract into your network, you also need to consider who the customers are who you want to attract to your brand. So when you use the tools of networking, you are using them in a way that creates attraction and in language that resonates with the people you want to attract.

Using social networking to market your brand is more about marketing *through* your network than *to* your network. Here are some tips on how to do it.

## Demonstrate competence

Social networks give you a much more accessible outlet than the media to demonstrate your expertise and competence. Start with ensuring your profile supports your brand story. Then contribute: speak up in a mailing list, message board, discussion forum or blog. Say something useful, original or profound, and you will get quoted and linked to by others. It's the number of people talking about you, quoting you, linking to you and referring you that creates your reputation and determines your competence.

### Rookie Buster

It's the number of people talking about you, quoting you, linking to you and referring you that creates your reputation and determines your competence.

## Give quality content

Whenever you write a post, add a comment, share information or offer advice or support, think about how that can subtly demonstrate your expertise without over-promoting yourself. Giving generously of your knowledge creates great attraction and leads others to investigate your profile.

## Build and reinforce your brand

Every signature in an email, on your posts and on your profiles online is an opportunity to reinforce your brand. You can make good use of signatures without forcing information on people.

## Ignite word-of-mouth buzz

If you have a new product or service, or if you are looking to build your reputation, satisfied customers talking about you is one of the most effective ways to establish your competence. Word-of-mouth flows through social networks; leaders of networks and groups are excellent

130 advocates. Get to know the most prominent blogger in your field. If they like what you sell or do, you will create a powerful supporter.

## Pull, don't push

Focus on creating awareness, not on persuasion. Your participation, your signatures, and your profiles will create awareness. Those who are interested will be attracted to you and will come to you for information and assistance.

## Link and cross-promote

Make sure that you link to your website in your email signature, your blog and your profiles, and to your communities from your website (and vice versa). Where there is an opportunity to link back to your presence on the internet, make use of it.

## Create a community around a cause or topic associated with your brand

Music groups, films, and authors can often support a community around their brand. However, it isn't always easy to create a fan base around your product or service. Instead you can build a community around a cause, as Avon does with its Breast Cancer Crusade or Dove with its Campaign for Real Beauty.

# Be consistent, not persistent

Online communication cannot be turned on and off like an advertising campaign. Online networks are generally not very receptive to immediate marketing messages from brand new members, nor to members who participate only when they are trying to sell something. You must earn the right to talk about your product through participation in and contribution to the community. It's all about building relationships and dialogue.

**Rookie Buster**

You must earn the right to talk about your product through participation in and contribution to the community.

# Find your niche groups

Within every network there are groups of people with particular interests they share or problems they want to solve. Frequent those relevant groups to participate and contribute your expertise; a ready-made target audience awaits you there. If it doesn't already exist or you can't find a board, list, chatroom or site with the exact focus you want, consider starting one of your own. While hosting one of these communities certainly takes time and effort, it will also put you in the centre of the network that forms around it, instead of on the periphery.

# Discussion lists

These are like bulletin boards, but are emailed on a regular basis to members of the list. When posting to these lists, you can include more information about yourself in a signature box at the end of each email.

Keep it short and include some reason for people to get in touch with you outside the list, such as "Subscribe to my free newsletter" or "Visit my website for a free resource guide." You can find discussion lists through search engines or through online community hosts such as Yahoo groups or MSN groups.

## Articles

Writing articles as a thought leader in your field and submitting them to online article banks such as www.ezinearticles.com or www.about. com should be a part of your marketing strategy if you want to build your reputation in your industry. Also, research your area of expertise on article sites, and notice who is writing them and who is being written about. These people are likely to be leaders in your field, or at least highly visible, which also makes them good networking contacts for you. Make contact with them, complimenting them on the article and suggesting you get acquainted for mutual benefit. Make a specific suggestion about what you can offer, such as referrals or resources.

## Blogs

Don't underestimate the power of your blog in raising your profile and getting yourself known. Regularly posting on frequently asked questions in your area of expertise and commenting on what is happening in your industry goes a long way to create the attraction you want in order to pull your customers to you. (Chapter 6 covers blogging in greater detail.)

## Using Twitter for business and marketing

Twitter is the latest of the social networking tools, and already there are others coming online that do a similar job. "Twitterers" can send

messages that are published either publicly or privately in a shared
environment. Anyone with access to this environment can follow the
flow of messages and comment, reply or simply keep up to date.

As with most social networking tools, Twitter started as a means for
kids to keep up to date instantaneously with what their friends were
doing, but it has become another – some would say essential – marketing tool in the kit for businesses. We mentioned following Twitter for
research purposes earlier in this chapter. Twitter can also be used in a
multitude of ways for pushing your message out as well as listening in
to others. It may or may not be for you, but it is worth investigating.

Nikki Pilkington (www.businessontwitter.co.uk) is a staunch advocate of Twittering for business. In July 2008 she wrote on her blog: "In
the past seven days I have:

- Generated 400+ signups to receive the 299 Steps to Website
  Heaven ebook for free on August 1st.
- Generated 50 downloads of a free Google Adwords ebook (today
  alone).
- Gained 2 new customers for my higher Google listings service.
- Gained feedback on 2 new business ideas (an online course and a
  day-by-day blog featuring the optimization of a website).
- Followed a link to get free promotional magnets for my company.
- Found out about 2 web conferences I wouldn't have known about
  otherwise.
- Promoted a client's article, which was then picked up by
  StumbledUpon and received over 400 visitors.
- Been offered a column in a holiday industry related magazine.
- Had industry news come to me, instead of me having to go out
  and find it."

Nikki also reports having pulled in significant amounts of revenue
from business generated just from her "twitterings" about what she
does. She isn't the only one, so clearly it has value as a marketing tool.
The advantage of Twitter is that is instant and quick, short and sweet,
and, because it is two-way, your customer has a chance to ask questions, maybe even place an order, and give feedback, all in real time.

134    In marketing terms Twitter is best used for tracking and directing attention. It allows you to monitor how influencers think or feel, and you can also actively network with them to gain their attention. Twitter is another networking channel that connects current and potential customers with your product or brand, which can help to build brand loyalty.

### Rookie Buster

Twitter is another networking channel that connects current and potential customers with your product or brand, which can help to build brand loyalty.

   Twitter can be seen as a traffic generation tool. The placement of links within profiles and conversations can direct visitors to a specific website and is especially powerful if your target audience are early adopters and influencers, as these are the people who are also Twittering. If your target audience are mature users who like tried and tested products that have been around for centuries, you aren't likely to find them on Twitter (though you could ask for referrals from other Twitterers who might know such people). This is why it is so crucial to know who your customer is – there's no point in wasting your marketing efforts and time talking to the wrong audience.

   For this reason, Twitter is not the best targeted lead acquisition tool, because it doesn't always reach the audience you want. Most Twitter users are somewhat web savvy, and it is difficult to target specific subsets of the general Twitter population and determine their level of potential interest.

   The main benefits of using Twitter as a marketing tool include:

- Creating another platform for building your personal brand, and establishing you as a social personality who is connected and approachable. Sending out mini-tips via Twitter or directing followers to your website/blog/articles for the full version is another way of directing traffic to your expertise.

- Directing customers/colleagues/friends to your website through clickable links within the Twitter messages. If you ask your friends to tweet about you too, the message will spread faster and further as other active users pick it up. There is a viral nature to all types of news, even on a site like Twitter. Do make sure you are spreading good quality information, though, as you'll quickly lose followers and friends if your messages are pointless or inane.
- Using Twitter as a social network for you to interact with other like-minded people, especially those in the same industry. It can be used to establish consistent and deeper relationships for future benefits such as testimonials or referrals.
- Performing rapid market research or simply asking for advice or feedback by sending a question out. Other users will reply, and this collective intelligence can be used in myriad ways.
- Keeping new and potential customers informed about forthcoming product updates. Existing customers like to know about products and services before everyone else. Build a loyal following by leaking them exclusive information.
- Offering customers the option of signing up to your Twitter campaign when they buy your product or services. This connects you with customers who are already actively interested in hearing more about what you have to offer, and completely avoids wasting your budget on the uninterested. Twitterers actively choose to "Follow" a flow of messages.
- Customers don't even need to be connected to the internet in order to receive your promotional messages. Once they register their mobile phone, they can receive updates via text.
- Keeping up with relevant news. Twitter users often link to useful sites or articles and can be a source of scoops and alternative news. You can also subscribe to Twitter feeds for specific websites or conferences, which allows you to receive and view content quickly. This is really useful if you want to be the first to make topical and timely comment on something happening in your industry.

## Coach's notes

**Three smart steps to knowing your customers (before you embark on a mega marketing campaign!)**

### 1. Get to know your customers

The best place to start is offline with existing customers, because you already have a relationship with them. This is what you want to know:

- What is important to them about your product or service?
- How did they decide to buy your product or service over the competition?
- How do they decide to keep buying yours over the competition?
- What do you give them that they feel is unique to you?
- Ask them to describe how they use or consume your product or service – you want their stories as to how it fits into their life; what problem you solve or need you fulfil.
- Is there anything about the experience of interacting with you or your company that is a turn-off for them? (Brave question, but you can't address it if you don't know.)
- Where do they go to get information about products or services such as yours? (Magazines, newspapers, websites, social networks, TV, radio?)
- Where would they definitely not go for information?
- If they were to sum up your "brand" in a few words, what words would they use?
- Will they give you a testimonial?

I suggest you have about six individual and in-depth discussions with existing customers, and record the conversations if possible (and with their permission). That way you can review the recording afterwards for things you may have missed, and you also can pay full attention to your customer without having to take notes. If you do nothing else I have advised in this book, do this. It will be the most useful thing you have ever done for your business.

2. **Armed with this information, look at your brand, your story**
Is the story you thought you told, and that you are intending to tell, consistent with the feedback from your customers? Their experience of you is more accurate than your own perception of yourself, so if you need to adjust your story or your brand position, do it.

Business is no longer just about transactions, it's about experiences and relationships. It's possible your customers may prefer a competitor's product but love the experience they get with you, so they stick with you rather than go elsewhere. This is so important to know, because it's that experience that is your story, and that story is what you should be spreading throughout your social network (and of course you can work on improving the product too).

Write down your story (your "brand proposition" in marketing speak) – what you will tell the world about the experience your customers can expect when they buy you, your product or service.

Bonus note: Look at every aspect of your business communications from your stationery to your website. Are they conveying the story? If not, take one step at a time and change them until they do.

3. **What are the commonalities among your customers?**
Are they of similar age, gender, interests, social groups, etc.? You are looking for clues to help you decide how best to find other people like them who could also become your customers, because in your social networking activities you need to:
- Identify the people who you want to attract.

- Tell your story in a way that will attract them.
- Enable others to recognize those people and refer them to you.
- Plus, when asking for referrals, know exactly who you are asking to be referred to; in other words, "Who do you know who has xxxx need/problem and would like to have xxxx [your story] experience instead?"

So now you know who your customers are, their commonalities, and what experience they truly value in you/your product/service that forms your story/brand proposition. Now you can decide how best to use social networking to reach these people. What will be the best mix of activities for you? The ones that enable you to engage in conversations with existing and potential customers, and with people who can refer or recommend you to the customers you want to attract.

**Go for it!** The most successful ideas and messages are shared when people are able to relate to them on their own terms, through their own experience, within their own map of the world. Information becomes cold, inert and impersonal data unless it is framed in a way that is *relevant to the experiences* of the recipient. Do you want what you have to offer to be perceived as cold data? No, you want a high-impact story that leaves a strong impression on your audience, so they'll pass it on to others in their network, who will then do the same. You have a high-impact story to tell; just ask your best customer, and they'll tell you what it is.

Notes

I have to admit that when I first came across social bookmarking a couple of years ago, I couldn't work out the purpose of it beyond being able to find web pages again that I particularly liked and found useful. If I wanted to refer a friend to a web page, I'd copy the URL and paste it into an email for them. However, as I started researching more into the notion of bookmarking, and noticing what others were doing with it, I realized that it has a much greater potential than just saving links. Sending and receiving content from friends is a great way to socialize and deepen online relationships and connections. Sharing appropriate information of interest can be a facilitator to conversations and dialogue with contacts with whom you don't yet have a strong relationship. It can also help build those relationships because it gives you a point of interest to share without having to "say" very much. This chapter will give you an overview of some of the many social bookmarking sites and how to use them to build relationships with your network and build your online presence.

# CHAPTER 9

# Building on your network through social bookmarking

## *Just what is social bookmarking?*

Social bookmarking is the practice of saving bookmarks to a public website, which allows users to qualify content; in other words, each "bookmark" of a specific web page is seen as a vote of confidence for that website. The more people who bookmark a specific web page, the more credible the webpage is perceived to be. In addition to bookmarking a web page, users "tag" the web page. The tags are simply single-word keywords that relate to the contents of the web page, making it easier to categorize and classify the content of the page. If everyone bookmarking a page uses similar keyword tags, the web page will be classified as a credible resource in a specific category.

As a web page receives more and more bookmarks from different users, the listing for the web page becomes more prominent in the listings. Users can bookmark and tag multiple pages within a website. Content can be tagged with multiple terms. As more users tag the content, it becomes easier to find similar topics.

Social bookmarking differs from general bookmarking (which is the practice of saving the address of a website you wish to visit in the

144 future on your computer, usually in your web browser) because it makes your bookmarked list visible to others. It is also of more use to you if you work from different locations or on more than one computer, because it keeps all your tagged web pages in one easily accessible place, and you don't have to remember which computer they are on!

Social bookmarking opens the door to new ways of organizing information and categorizing resources. Social bookmarking sites indicate who created each bookmark and provide access to that person's other bookmarked resources, so you can easily make social connections with others who are interested in similar topics. You can see how many people have used a tag and search for all resources that have been assigned that tag.

## Rookie Buster

Social bookmarking sites indicate who created each bookmark and provide access to that person's other bookmarked resources, so you can easily make social connections with others who are interested in similar topics.

So you can save your favourite websites in a location that you can always access on the web, you can send links to friends, and you can browse through other web pages that others have found interesting enough to tag. Most sites allow you to browse for "most popular", "recently added", or tags belonging to a certain category such as shopping, technology, politics, blogging, news, sports, etc. You can even search through what people have bookmarked by typing into the search tool what you are looking for.

In this way social bookmarking sites are being used as intelligent    145
search engines. Social news tracking is a form of social bookmarking,
but focuses on specific news items and blog posts rather than websites
in general.

**Rookie Buster**

Social bookmarking sites are being used as intelligent
search engines.

## *How you can benefit from social bookmarking*

Social bookmarking allows you to specifically target what you want to
see. Instead of going into a search engine, typing something in, and
then trawling through the results to find the one website with the best
bits of information, you can quickly narrow down the items to what
you are looking for. Many social bookmarking sites display recently
added lists and popular links, so you can both stay current and see
relevant information. Plus, because the articles have votes, it's pretty
easy to tell that an article with a hundred votes might be a better choice
than one with three votes. You no longer need to page through thousands of results to find the one article that you really want.

It doesn't take a great leap of imagination then to realize that if your
website or blog is bookmarked and voted on as popular, you will be
easy to find via social bookmarking. We all tend to rely on or seek
recommendations for everything from books to business associates,
and social bookmarks are the latest route to referrals and recommendations. How do you get yourself linked to? By providing good quality
content that is useful and shares your expertise. You can also ask your
colleagues and contacts to link to you; however, you need to be careful
about requesting reciprocal links or reviews, as some sites expressly

146    forbid this and will eject you if you do it. Always check the terms and rules of the site you are planning to use. In any case don't explicitly ask for a review if you don't know the other person well. Let them decide if they want to bookmark the webpage too – or not.

**Rookie Buster**

You need to be careful about requesting reciprocal links or reviews, as some sites expressly forbid this and will eject you if you do it.

Most social bookmarking sites have a function where you can send pages to others. This is a useful way of keeping your networks in touch with articles or web pages of interest, and of course your own articles, blog posts and website updates. Do not send every single article you write on your website to everyone you know! This can be irritating, particularly if the reader in question is already subscribed to your site. Regulate your frequency by sending web pages to different users, or by sending only your best articles.

Similarly don't use your social bookmarking account to reference only your own web pages. You'll gain greater credibility by sharing different content. Share interesting videos, pictures and other interesting content, or use the send-to feature to enquire about a specific topic.

Relevance is crucial. Only send articles that you know will interest the person in question. The only way to know this for sure is to go beyond their avatar to examine what they bookmark, while taking note of their website or listed interests.

Most sites also enable you to add comments to the link you are sending or bookmarking. Take advantage of this space, because it gives you a chance to say why you are recommending this link, and enables you to slip in something about yourself or your business in the context of that link. Comments also add a personal touch to the sharing process, and you should definitely use them to share your thoughts

and feelings. If someone sends you a page with a comment, reply with     147
a comment too; it's a quick way to get a brief conversation going.

## How to "meet" people on social bookmarking sites

This is just another form of social networking. Having joined a particular site, you can search through the public bookmarks and, as you find interesting websites, make note of the user who added the bookmark. You can view their profile, and browse through other bookmarks they have added. If their interests are aligned with yours, and you like the sites they have bookmarked, you can add them as a friend.

## Social bookmarking for your own marketing and PR

Marketing these days is much less about pushing a message "out there" and more about pulling potential customers to you. They come because they trust you. They trust you because they feel they know you. They think they know you because they feel you have some shared synergy or interest, or knowledge that they need. The real value in social bookmarking as a marketing or PR tool therefore is not in pushing your own web pages so much as being a source and a connector to all the best information that your readers (or the press) could want on your area of expertise.

If you are looking to build your personal profile and reputation via the internet, being the fount of all knowledge is a good way to get started and build quickly. You may not have time to write tons of blog posts on your subject, or you may not feel you are much of a writer, but if you can read, bookmark and tag the writing of others, and add insightful but short comments to your bookmarks, then you can fairly quickly appear to be someone who knows their subject and therefore is worth paying attention to.

**Rookie Buster**

If you are looking to build your personal profile and reputation via the internet, being the fount of all knowledge is a good way to get started and build quickly.

Social bookmarking sites are, by virtue of being a means of gathering information, an excellent source for market research. Because all posts are tagged, just searching on a keyword for your area of interest brings up all the links under that tag. You can then see clearly what the hot topics are in your area of interest, what is being discussed, what thoughts and feedback are shared and who are the most followed writers in this field. You can find out what customers are saying and how they are saying it; what is important to them, what they love and what they hate. Imagine being able to include in your proposal to a prospective client a selection of relevant quotes from their customers sourced from your social bookmarking research. How impressive might that be? It is quite easy to do – the information is out there if you just go and look.

# An overview of social bookmarking sites

Most social bookmarking/news sites work in similar ways. You sign up for an account and submit content in the form of links to web pages, videos, podcasts or blogs. Other members of the site then vote (usually by adding it to their list too) and comment, and the submissions that get the most votes rise up the rankings, and if they are really popular they make the front page. As with social networking sites, there are a huge number of bookmarking sites available. Those listed here are some of the most popular, but the list is by no means exhaustive, and you will need to look at the various sites to see which suits you best. As with networking, you can join a number of different bookmarking sites to increase your visibility.

## Social news sites
Digg (www.digg.com)
Newsvine (www.newsvine.com)
Reddit (www.reddit.com)

## General social bookmarking sites
Blinklist (www.blinklist.com)
Delicious (www.delicious.com)
Furl (www.furl.net)
Ma.gnolia (www.ma.gnolia.com)
Mixx (www.mixx.com)
Propeller (www.propeller.com)
StumbleUpon (www.stumbleupon.com)
Yahoo Buzz (www.buzz.yahoo.com)

## Video sharing sites
These work like any other social bookmarking sites, except that they focus on uploaded videos.
Tubearoo (www.tubearoo.com)
YouTube (www.youtube.com)

## Sites for increasing visibility of your expertise
Squidoo (www.squidoo.com). According to Squidoo, "Everyone's an expert on something." It is slightly different to the other sites in that you create a "lens" – a single web page – through which you share your knowledge, your passions or your industry's secrets. You can have multiple lenses, but each lens has its own subject, and the page can be as long as you want it to be.

Technorati (www.technorati.com). If you want to increase your blog's readership, consider registering it with Technorati, a network of blogs and writers that lists top stories in categories like business, entertainment and technology.

WikiHow (www.wikihow.com). This is a good place to write a how-to guide or tutorial to share your knowledge, or to contribute to other articles.

Coach's notes

**Getting started with your bookmarks**

1. Decide on what you want your social bookmarking activity to do for you. Do you want:
   - Just an accessible list of web pages for your own reference?
   - A means of building up a databank of information sources to share with friends and colleagues?
   - To build your reputation and profile by being the source of knowledge and thought leader in your field?

2. Investigate the many options available. These range from Delicious, one of the oldest and most popular sites, to Blinklist, an excellent choice for beginners, to Ma.gnolia, which specializes in community-building features. Most social bookmarking sites allow you to search through the public bookmarks as a guest. The best way to find out which one is right for you is to actually use the site. Search through the bookmarks, see if the look-and-feel appeals to you, and determine whether or not you find the site easy to use.

3. Once you have picked a social bookmarking site, you will want to install a button on to your browser to make it easy to use. The site should provide a tutorial on installing the button, either after you sign up or in their help section.

4. Once you have your account set up and have the button installed, you are ready to start bookmarking websites. Simply go to whatever website you want to bookmark, and click the button in your browser. Most sites will either pop up a small window, or take you to their site and ask you a few questions about the website you are bookmarking. It should fill out some of the information for you, like the title and the website address.

5. Create your tag for that page or link. Your tag is a keyword or phrase used to describe the website. Think of it like the name of a folder. You can also have multiple tags, which can be very handy. For example, if you are bookmarking a blog about

social media marketing, you might tag it "social media", "marketing", "blog" and the name of the blogger.

Because you used multiple tags, you can now find the bookmarks in multiple ways. If you always tag your favourite blogs with the tag of "blog", you can pull up all of your blogs by just typing in that keyword. Or you could pull up all the pages you have tagged under "social media", or pages you have tagged from a particular blogger. It makes your bookmarked pages easier to find.

6. Depending on the social bookmarking site, you might also have a "tag cloud". A tag cloud is a list of tags, with the most popular tags receiving a bigger and/or bolder font than tags that are not as popular. Tag clouds allow you to quickly pick out your most popular bookmarks, and to see the most popular bookmarks of others. You'll recognize the tag cloud when you see a group of words all in different sizes and weights on one side of the web page.

7. Add your comments. Make sure you make good use of the comment box. You can state why you think that particular page or link is important, or indeed why you think it is giving poor information and is not a trustworthy source, if you believe that to be the case. You can add insights, thoughts and opinions – and if your strategy is to build your reputation as a thought leader, then you definitely should add your insights and opinions. You can also reference to your own product or service as relevant (but it must genuinely be relevant, and not just a sales pitch!). For example, let's say you are bookmarking an article in which your product is featured among others and it gets a favourable review – you might say in your comment that this article gave a good overview of the products available in that category and you are delighted that your own product was highly recommended.

**Go for it!** If you are using social bookmarking as an extension of your network, then, as with all aspects of social networking, you have to think in terms of "what would I say" and "how would I behave" if this person was standing in front of you. Noticing that someone happened to bookmark the same link as you might merit a "hello" as the equivalent of an introductory handshake, but equally it might not. Look beyond that one bookmarking action to their other bookmarks: is there a shared interest? If there is, then a personalized message might be a good opportunity to break the ice. If not, then move on. If they bookmarked your own web page, you might send a "thank you", but don't take it as an opportunity to bombard them with more messages. Always look for shared interest or synergy.

*Notes*

Social networking online is a great way of expanding your contacts base and getting to know people who you wouldn't otherwise have met. However, the best relationships, and the most likely opportunities for business, still come when you get to know each other away from the online platform. Online networks help build your profile and your reputation, and are the conduit to initiating and managing relationships, but they aren't a complete substitute for meeting face to face. The business opportunities may be initiated online, but the deal is usually sealed in person. We do business with people whom we trust, and we trust those with whom we have built up a relationship; so online networks should be seen as a means to an end, not the end in itself.

CHAPTER 10

# The best relationships are developed offline too!

## *How do you get the best out of offline networking?*

Many of the online business networks actively encourage or even facilitate meetings of local members and one-to-one meetings. Going to these meetings can be useful for expanding your network and building relationships with people you have already met online. Equally there are many business networking groups in most localities, and you can keep in touch with people you meet at these events through your online networks – if they aren't a member, invite them to join.

**Rookie Buster**

The best relationships, and most likely opportunities for business, still come when you get to know each other away from the online platform.

## 156 Choosing offline networks

As with online networks, networking offline can be even more time consuming, particularly as you now have to take into consideration travel, time out from your day and the need to dress appropriately. Therefore you need to think carefully about what networks are available locally and nationally, and which suit your needs best. Is your strategy to build a wide network of random connections, or a deep network of managed relationships? Do you need to build up your connections and reputation in a specific industry or in a geographical location? Are you looking to meet small business owners or specific managers in large corporates? Are you looking to develop your own business or to move up the corporate career ladder? All these considerations have an impact on the networks you choose to attend.

Networking is about business development, not sales; unfortunately many people attending networking events haven't got this message yet. It's not about how many business cards you can hand out, it's about getting to know people and their expertise, and them getting to know about you.

## Networking can happen anywhere

Networking opportunities come in many forms: parties, dinners, weddings, alumni functions, conferences, social and sporting events, church. You don't have to attend a networking event to network. Even sitting next to someone on a train can give you the opportunity to strike up a conversation.

**Rookie Buster**

You don't have to attend a networking event to network.

Whatever event you are attending, walking into a room full of    157
people can be intimidating, even when you know some of them. Look
for those you know, and approach them first to build confidence, then
ask them to introduce you to someone you don't know but who they
think is interesting. Look for open groups of twos and threes; open
groups are those who are at right angles to each other, rather than
standing face to face and engrossed in deep conversation.

## Plan your performance

It may seem an odd thing to be planning, but if you have not attended
the network or event before, a bit of research beforehand is sensible
and may even be critical. You don't want to turn up to an event thinking it's an informal social to find it's actually a formal event with a
specific format, and that you're arriving at the wrong time and dressed
inappropriately.

Here are some points to check:

- What is the format?
- What are the exact timings – not just the start time, but the
  running order of the event?
- Where it is? Make sure you know how to get there; getting lost
  can take longer than you think!
- What is the dress code?
- What topics are appropriate to talk about?

## Dress appropriately

At official networking events, dress like you
mean business. First impressions count, so
make sure you present yourself in a confident
manner that will encourage others to take you
seriously. At the same time, you need to dress for
comfort and confidence, and decide whether you want
to stand out or fit in. Jeans are not acceptable

158    everywhere, but if you are in the creative world of art and design, they
may be the standard dress. You can stand out by wearing a suit and tie,
or fit in by wearing your jeans too. Whatever you wear, make it appropriate for the occasion, clean, ironed, smart and not too revealing. You
want the attention on you and your expertise.

### Rookie Buster

First impressions count, so make sure you present
yourself in a confident manner that will encourage others
to take you seriously.

## Be approachable and approach others too

It may feel intimidating, but remember that everyone is there for the
same reason. If you feel shy, approach someone who is standing alone
and strike up a conversation; they will be very grateful that you made
the first move. Equally, if you are standing alone, don't stare into your
wine glass, but look like you are just taking a break between conversations and be open to approaches.

## Don't go for the hard sell

Networking is not selling; it's about building and nurturing business
relationships. Ask for advice or offer it. Find common areas of interest
or ask about their life outside work. You may not get immediate business opportunities; networking provides the chance to meet new
people and for you to get to know and trust each other over time.

 **Rookie Buster**

Networking is not selling; it's about building and nurturing business relationships.

## Develop your small talk

Being able to talk to anyone about anything is a valuable skill. Questions like "How did you get started in this business?" and "Tell me about your background," or even "What do you like to do outside work?" open the door for a longer conversation. People love to talk about themselves and express their opinions. Always listen more than you talk: not only does this make the other person feel more appreciated, but you get much more information on which to build the relationship.

## Stop asking "What do you do?"

Just about every networking event you go to, the first question is "What do you do?" The advantage with online networking is that your profile has already given that information (or should have), so the conversation starts at a different place. A better question might be "What's your area of expertise?", or "What projects are you working on right now?" Or you might ask "Do you attend this network regularly?" or even "Why do you choose to attend this network?" Make the question more interesting, and the answers will be too.

## Be interested and interesting

You never know who someone may know or how they may be able to help you, so always remember to make an effort to be interested in

160     everyone, even if they may not seem to be of immediate "use". Be interesting too – don't bore people with industry talk, and have a stash of topics up your sleeve that you can engage people with, such as an interesting book, TV programme or place to visit.

## Be helpful

Do you have a contact that would benefit their business? Can you recommend a good book that might interest them? People always remember someone who has been helpful, so you never know when they might repay the favour one day.

### Rookie Buster

People always remember someone who has been helpful, so you never know when they might repay the favour one day.

## Work the room

Don't spend the whole event with one person. Introduce yourself to as many people as you can, and encourage others to do the same. Don't be afraid to politely end the conversation and move on, or introduce them to someone else so that you can move on. If you are ready to move on, make sure your body language is open to invite others to approach you and join in the conversation.

## Alternatively don't work the room

There are some occasions when not working the room is a better option, particularly at purely social events, when you often find that the room works itself. At events that have a common theme – concerts, conferences, parties and so on – you usually find yourself talking to someone apparently randomly, but with whom you later build a strong relationship, or there are introductions that you can offer them or they you. Networking is not just a task to be undertaken; sometimes you can just allow the connections to come to you.

## Keep in touch

Keep track of any business cards that you have collected and make sure you always follow up any contacts that might be beneficial via email or a quick phone call. It may be just to say that it was nice to meet them and to offer to help in any way you can. Even if there is nothing you can do for them (or that they can do for you) immediately, an opportunity may arise in the future.

It is often the long-term relationships that you make, nurture and develop that can make a huge difference for you. You can't necessarily measure the strength of your connections based on the immediate benefits you derive from them. The relationship may only come into its own after some years, when you are both in much higher positions and have built other connections of mutual benefit. But if you hadn't nurtured that relationship, where would you be?

The absolute key to building your networks online or offline lies in realizing that networking is not just an activity, but it's a group of connections and relationships that you build, and those connections can come from anywhere, at any time. Joining a network or attending a networking event is just one means to building those connections.

**Rookie Buster**

It is often the long-term relationships that you make, nurture and develop that can make a huge difference for you.

# 162 *Taking your online networking offline*

No matter how strong a connection you have made with your network contacts online, at some point you will feel the compulsion to meet in person, to take the relationship to the next level of connection and trust. You just get a much stronger impression of who someone is, of whether you like them, trust them and want to do business with them, if you have spent some time in their company. Meeting one to one or even in a small group is definitely recommended as the way to nurture and build those relationships.

Meeting face to face with your contacts is extremely important for many reasons. You get far more than just their work history and expertise, you start to learn more about who they are –their values, beliefs and experiences, and their world. And they get to learn about you. This is not a time to sell your services; the people you meet are not your market, they are your potential *route* to market. This is the time for informal chat. You have an opportunity here to put across a clear impression of who you really are, as well as your expertise and what you offer. You must extend the same opportunity to them. They are more likely to want to refer or recommend you, if they feel you truly understand them too.

Rory Murray gives good advice on this on his blog www.returnonrelationships.net: "It becomes especially important when you meet somebody who either has a complex business proposition, or hasn't yet worked out how to explain their proposition clearly and concisely. By taking the time to understand it, you achieve at least two things – you have clarity about who they are and what they do (which means you can refer them more easily), you help them understand what's important to others (which means they will do a better job of explaining their business proposition next time), and you probably become more memorable and

valuable to them for just taking the time (which means they will find     163
it easier to refer you)."

It is important to be yourself too. You know that when someone tries to impress you, it often comes across as too forced or incongruent. Sometimes you don't even know why, but there is something off-putting about that person. You wonder why they are trying so hard. Of course you won't always get on so well with someone that you forget the time and coffee turns into lunch, but that is more likely to happen if you are both relaxed and being yourselves, rather than trying to be impressive. The best relationships in all spheres of life are those where you do not have to compromise on who you are.

Talk about your life and experiences, and ask about theirs. Listen more than talk. Do ask how you might be able to assist them right now, but don't interrogate them or pitch your needs too heavily. Sadly that just comes across as desperate and inappropriate. All of us need help, and at times we need more help than at others; there is a fine line between asking for help and pleading for it. If you felt under pressure to help them, you would most likely feel like backing away from the relationship. The old adage "Do as you would be done unto" is very appropriate in this world of building relationships.

### Rookie Buster

The old adage "Do as you would be done unto" is very appropriate in this world of building relationships.

If you aren't finding any common ground and the conversation is hard work, don't be afraid of cutting the meeting short. If it's hard work for you, it's probably hard work for them too. We've all been there – you get on like a house on fire on your email exchanges, but you just don't click when you meet. Make sure you have given them the opportunity to explain what they do and the types of people they want to meet, and to feel "heard". Then quietly close the meeting and move on.

164    Another important thing that is often forgotten in informal meetings is to switch the mobile off, or at least on to silent. There is nothing
more irritating and credibility-destroying than your mobile phone
going off incessantly – or even worse, your answering it incessantly! It's
not just rude, it sends a clear message to the other person that they just
aren't that important. It may seem like preaching the obvious, but you
would be surprised by the number of people who just answer their
phones oblivious to how that affects the other person and the relationship they were trying to build. Treat this as an important meeting, even
if it is an informal one, because it is. This person might be the key connector for your business success.

Your aim in meeting your online connections face to face is to build
on your understanding of who they are, what they stand for, their
expertise and what you can contribute to them or their network. The
purpose of the meeting is to build your relationship with them, so that
you can grow to like, trust and respect each other. You should aim to
leave the meeting with an understanding of each other and your
respective businesses, so that you feel comfortable in recommending
or referring each other to your networks when an opportunity arises.
This is equally the case whether you are networking with others inside
or outside your industry, within your company or externally with
other peers.

## Networking within organizations

Most people think of networking – business or social – as being solely
external networking with people you don't know, but a huge opportunity that is frequently missed is to network within your organization,
particularly if you work in a large company where departments tend
to segregate themselves into their particular disciplines or offices and
not talk to others. How many times have you heard someone say that
"Oh, that's the marketing team's thing, we don't talk to each other," or
similar?

## Rookie Buster

A huge opportunity that is frequently missed is to network within your organization.

If you stick within your peer group and don't talk to other departments and people in your organization, you are limiting the size and quality of your network. There are many people you may not meet; people who will never be able to refer or recommend you because they will never get the chance to know, like and trust you. Why would you reduce the chances of getting referrals, recommendations, promotion or repeat business?

If you are a contractor, consultant or supplier to a large organization, who else might need your services at some point in the future? Is your relationship with your direct client strong enough to ask for a referral to others in the organization – not necessarily for immediate business opportunities, but to add to your network? If it isn't, then what can you do to strengthen it? If you're recognized as someone who does a great job, or has an area of expertise that is crucial to the business, then your client or your company will want to retain you. It's much easier to get more business from existing clients, and it's much easier to get promotion or a pay rise with an existing employer – but only if they know about you, your expertise and your value to them. Internal networking increases your value.

Sharing your knowledge freely (but judiciously) within the organization helps your colleagues, peers, managers and so on to see how knowledgeable you are. As always, you must be wary of conflicts of interest and jeopardizing intellectual property, but with that in mind,

166      sharing your expertise and knowledge, helping others and making a contribution within the organization will enhance your reputation and raise both your visibility and credibility. So when it comes to promotion or repeat business, who is going to be first in line? The person who is visible and credible or the one who is invisible (regardless of their credibility)? It's a no-brainer. If you are getting passed over for promotion and you really are good at your job, then get networking and increase your visibility.

**The only time you can pitch – and you have 60 seconds, starting now!**

Some networking organizations and events give all attendees a 60-second slot to pitch their business; some give a slot to names drawn out of a hat. This is sometimes known in American jargon as the "elevator pitch" – because it is what you would say if you had the undivided attention of someone in an elevator for 30 to 60 seconds and they asked you about your business. Sometimes it is known as a 60-second "introduction". Either way, it is the one time you can blatantly pitch your business at a networking event, and you should have your pitch honed and toned in your mind so that you can deliver it elegantly and eloquently if called on to do so.

It is also the one thing that most people struggle with; how to sum up your business in four sentences at most? Prepare yours in answer to these four questions – a short one-sentence answer for each:

- What is my service or product?
- What problem do I solve (or what need do I fulfil)?
- How am I different?
- What is in it for you?

Think about using words that are concise, clear (use language that everyone understands), powerful and visual (words that create a visual image in your listeners' minds).

Think about it as a short story – a good story is usually about someone with a problem who either finds a solution or faces tragedy. How can you create a "happy ever after" for your audience?

Think about your hook – the "what's in it for them?" in a phrase they can remember you by. This phrase needs to strike a chord in your listener and make them want to know more.

It is worth putting time into developing this and keeping it in your wallet; you just never know when you are going to need it. And you don't want to be tongue-tied when you get that chance!

**Go for it!** The saying "It's not what you know, it's who you know" isn't quite accurate. More important is who knows *you*, and what they are saying about you when you aren't in the room. Are they extolling your virtues and recommending you highly, or do you not get much of a mention (or worse, do they suggest you are a great person but not reliable)? Your networks need to know you well enough to trust you and to want to help you, and they need to understand your business needs in enough depth to spot opportunities for you when they arise, whether or not you are aware of those opportunities at the time.

Whether those are opportunities for promotion within your organization, for new business, for repeat business or for connections that will be useful or interesting, what makes the difference is who knows, likes, trusts and respects you. That is why networking in all its forms should be such a key part of your life, and will be a key part of your success.

*Notes*

# Appendix

## Glossary of terms

**Aggregation** is the process of gathering and remixing content from blogs and other websites that provide RSS feeds. The results may be displayed in an aggregator website such as Bloglines or Google Reader, or directly on your desktop using software (often also called a newsreader).

**Alerts:** search engines allow you to specify words, phrases or tags that you want checked periodically, with results of those searches returned to you by email. You may also be able to read the searches by RSS feed. This form of search allows you to check whether you, your organization, your blog or blog item has been mentioned elsewhere, and so to respond if you wish.

**Archive** may refer to topics from an online discussion that has been closed but saved for later reference. On blogs, archives are collections of earlier items, usually organized by week or month.

**Authenticity** – it isn't always easy to tell who is "real" on the internet and who isn't. Blogs and social networks enable people to publish content, and engage in conversations, that show their interests and values, and so help them develop online authenticity.

**Avatars** are graphical images representing people. They are what you are in virtual worlds. You can build a visual character with the body, clothes, behaviours, gender and name of your choice. This may or may not be an authentic representation of yourself.

**Blogs** are websites with dated items of content in reverse chronological order, self-published by bloggers. Entries or posts may have keyword tags associated with them, are usually available as feeds, and often allow readers to comment.

**Blogger:** the writer of a blog.

**Blogosphere:** a term used to describe the vast number of blogs on the internet, and the conversations taking place between bloggers.

**Blogroll:** a list of sites displayed in the sidebar of blog, showing who the blogger reads or recommends.

**Bookmarking:** saving the address of a website or item of content, either in your browser, or on a social bookmarking site.

**Bulletin boards** were the early vehicles for online collaboration, where users connected with a central computer to post and read email-like messages. They were the electronic equivalent of public notice boards. The term is still used for forums.

**Categories:** pre-specified ways to organize content on a website or blog.

**Chat:** interaction on a website, with a number of people adding text items one after the other into the same space at (almost) the same time. A place for chat – a chat room – differs from a forum because conversations happen in "real time", rather as they do face to face.

**Collaboration:** being able to discuss and work with people across boundaries of organization, time and space. Activities like commenting, social bookmarking, chatting and blogging help develop the trust necessary for collaboration to be achieved.

**Comments:** bloggers may allow readers to add comments to their posts, and may also provide a feed for comments as well as for main items.

**Communities:** groups of people with shared interests communicating mainly through the internet.

**Community building:** the process of recruiting potential community or network participants, helping them to find shared interests and goals, use the technology, and develop useful conversations.

**Content:** text, pictures, video and any other meaningful material that is on the internet.

**Conversation** through blogging, commenting or contributing to forums is the currency of social networking.

**Copyright:** the right of an author for his work to remain his and not be used by another without permission. Maintaining copyright on the internet is more difficult than in print. The Creative Commons licence was created for this purpose and attaching such a licence to your work enables you to specify your copyright terms; for example, that content may be re-used with attribution, provided that a similar licence is then attached by the new author.

**Cyberspace** has been widely used as a general term for the internet or World Wide Web.

**Download:** to retrieve a file or other content from an internet site to your computer or other device.

**Email lists**, or groups, are important networking tools offering the facility to send a message from a central post box to any number of subscribers, and for them to respond. Internet marketers set great store by generating a huge email subscriber list, as this enables them to market frequently with new offers directly to their subscribers' inboxes.

**Facilitator:** someone who helps people in an online group or forum to manage their conversations. They may help agree a set of rules, draw out topics for discussion, gently keep people on topic, and summarize.

**Feeds:** the means by which you can read, view or listen to items from blogs and other RSS-enabled sites without visiting the site, by subscribing and using an aggregator or newsreader. Feeds contain the content of an item and any associated tags in plain text.

**Forums:** discussion areas on websites, where people can post messages or comment on existing messages.

**Friends:** contacts whose profiles you link to in your profile on social networking sites.

**Groups:** collections of individuals with shared activities, interests or values. They are bounded: you are either in a group or not. Groups differ in this from networks, which are not bounded and are defined by connections rather than interests.

**Instant messaging (IM)** is chat with one other person using an IM tool like AOL Instant Messenger, Microsoft Live Messenger or Yahoo Messenger. The tools allow you to indicate whether or not you are available for a chat, and if so can be a good alternative to emails for a rapid exchange.

**Links:** the highlighted text or images that, when clicked, jump you from one web page or item of content to another. Bloggers use links a lot when writing, to reference their own or other content. Linking is another aspect of sharing.

**Lurkers:** people who read but don't contribute or add comments to online communities.

**Networks:** structures defined by nodes and the connections between them. In social networks the nodes are people, and the connections are the relationships that they have. Networking is the process by which you develop and strengthen those relationships.

**Newsreader:** in the online world, a website or desktop tool that act as an aggregator, gathering content from blogs and similar sites using RSS feeds so that you can read the content in one place, instead of having to visit different sites.

**Open-source software:** Wikipedia offers this definition: "refers to any computer software whose source code is available under a licence that permits users to study, change, and improve the software, and to redistribute it in modified or unmodified form. It is often developed in a public, collaborative manner."

**Peer-to-peer:** refers to direct interaction between two people in a network.

**Permalink:** the address (URL) of an item of content, for example a blog post, rather than the address of a web page with lots of different items. You will often find it at the end of a blog post.

**Photo-sharing:** uploading your images to a website such as Flickr. You can add tags and offer people the opportunity to comment or even re-use your photos with an appropriate copyright licence.

**Podcast:** audio or video content that can be downloaded automatically through a subscription to a website so that you can view or listen offline.

**Post:** an item or entry on a blog or forum. "To post" is to add an entry to the blog or forum.

176    **Profiles:** the information that you provide about yourself when signing up for a social networking site. As well as a picture and basic information, this may include your personal and business interests, something about yourself, and tags to help people search for like-minded people.

**Registration:** the process of providing a username, password and other details when seeking to access a website that has restricted access.

**Remixing:** social media offers the possibility of taking different items of content, identified by tags and published through feeds, and combining them in different ways. You can do this with other people's content if they add an appropriate copyright licence.

**RSS:** Really Simple Syndication. This allows you to subscribe to content on blogs and other social media and have it delivered to you through a feed.

**Social media:** a term for the tools and platforms people use to publish, converse and share content online. The tools include blogs, wikis, podcasts and sites to share photos and bookmarks.

**Social networking sites** are online places where users can create a profile for themselves, and then socialize with others using a range of social media tools including blogs, video, images, tagging, lists of friends, forums and messaging.

**Subscribing:** the process of adding an RSS feed to your aggregator or newsreader. It can also be the process of adding your email address to a list held by a particular website owner or blogger – usually in return for free tips or newsletters.

**Tags:** keywords attached to a blog post, bookmark, photo or other item of content so that you and others can find them easily through searches and aggregation.

**Terms of services:** the basis on which you agree to use a forum or 177
other web-based place for creating or sharing content. Check before
agreeing what rights the site owners may claim over your content.

**Threads:** strands of conversation. On an email list or web forum they
will be defined by messages that use the same subject. On blogs
they are less clearly defined, but emerge through comments and
trackbacks.

**Tool:** used here as shorthand for a software application on your computer, and also for applications that are web-based.

**Topic:** an idea, issue or talking point in an online conversation that is
made up of threads.

**Trackback:** some blogs provide a facility for other bloggers to leave a
calling card automatically, instead of commenting. Blogger A may
write on blog A about an item on blogger B's site, and through the
trackback facility leave a link on B's site back to A. The collection of
comments and trackbacks on a site facilitates conversations.

**Upload:** to transfer a file or other content from your computer to an
internet site.

**URL:** Unique Resource Locator is the technical term for a web address
like http://www.bbc.co.uk.

**Virtual worlds:** online places like Second Life, where you can create a
representation of yourself (an avatar) and socialize with other residents. Basic activity is free, but you can buy currency (using real
money) in order to purchase land and trade with other residents.
Second Life is being used by some voluntary organizations to run
discussions, virtual events and fundraising.

**Voice Over Internet Protocol (VOIP)** enables you to use a computer
or other internet device for phone calls without additional charge,

178    including conference calls. By using headphones and a microphone you can also free your hands to use instant messaging to keep a shared note of conversations, or use other virtual presence tools. You can use Voice Over IP to do interviews for Podcasts. The best-known VOIP tool is Skype.

**Web 2.0:** a term coined by O'Reilly Media in 2004 to describe blogs, wikis, social networking sites and other internet-based services that emphasize collaboration and sharing, rather than less interactive publishing (or Web 1.0).

**Web-based tools:** Google, Yahoo and a host of other commercial organizations provide an increasing range of free or low-cost tools including email, calendars, word processing, and spreadsheets that can be used on the web rather than your desktop. Provided you are happy to entrust your data to these organizations – and are always online when working – you can reduce your software costs significantly and forget about upgrades.

**Widgets:** stand-alone applications that you can embed in other applications, such as a website or a desktop. These may help you to do things like subscribe to a feed, do a specialist search, or even make a donation.

A **wiki** is a web page – or set of pages – that can be edited collaboratively. The best-known example is Wikipedia, an encyclopedia created by thousands of contributors across the world. Once people have appropriate permissions – set by the wiki owner – they can create pages and/or add to and alter existing pages.

This list was drawn from:
http://socialmedia.wikispaces.com/A-Z+of+social+media

# *Resources* 179

The following is not an exhaustive list of resources, but is a list of sites that you may find useful for further research into social networking and social media marketing.

## Lists of social networks

http://findasocialnetwork.com/search.php
http://www.insidecrm.com/features/50-social-sites-012808/
http://traffikd.com/social-media-websites/
http://en.wikipedia.org/wiki/List_of_social_networking_websites

## Bloggers on networking, social networking and social media

www.businessontwitter.co.uk
www.doshdosh.com
www.linkedintelligence.com
www.networkingandreferrals.blogspot.com
www.pr-squared.com/jedi.html
www.publishing2.com
www.returnonrelationships.net
www.socialnetworking.thingstoknowonline.com
www.traffikd.com
www.web-strategist.com/blog
www.wordsofabrokenmirror.com

## Article sites

www.about.com
www.ezinearticles.com
Both of these have a large number of useful articles on social networking.

And of course you only have to put "social networking" into the search box of any social bookmarking site and it will come up more than enough pages to choose from!

# 180   *The flame and wax exercise (from Chapter 1)*

Imagine you are a candle — part of you is the flame, and part of you is the wax.

When you are in your flame, leveraging on your talents and your expertise, shining brightly in your sphere of influence, you light up the world around you, and people are attracted to that light. When you are in your wax, doing the stuff that needs doing but which doesn't light your fire, you don't feel so great, life feels heavy and your light dims.

Your flame consists of the talents, expertise and interests you have that other people will be attracted to and want to connect with. Your work should be making the most of these. Your wax contains the things that you might find help or support with in the connections you make. Where possible you should be outsourcing your wax activities. Remember that everyone's list will be different and what is your wax will be someone else's flame. They will love the tasks you hate! Networking will help you find the right people to share your expertise *and* your mundane tasks with.

Use this table to help you decide what is in each list; there are some examples to help you.

| **My flame** | **My wax** |
|---|---|
| *Examples:* | *Examples:* |
| Talking with people face to face | Keeping track of receipts |
| Writing articles | Keeping my contacts database up to date |
| Thinking creatively/problem solving | General admin tasks |
| Speaking to groups of any size | Cold calling by phone |
| Making others feel safe and comfortable | |

Have fun!

# Index